# PROCLAIMING THE TRUTH OF JESUS CHRIST

## PAPERS FROM THE VALLOMBROSA MEETING

UNITED STATES CATHOLIC CONFERENCE
WASHINGTON, D.C.

*Proclaiming the Truth of Jesus Christ: Papers from the Vallombrosa Meeting* is a compilation of printed essays originally prepared for the Vallombrosa Meeting held in Menlo Park, Calif., from February 9-12, 1999. The publishing of these essays was approved in August 1999 by the Congregation for the Doctrine of the Faith and the Committee on Doctrine. *Proclaiming the Truth of Jesus Christ* is authorized for publication by the undersigned.

BT
78
. P66
2000

Monsignor Dennis M. Schnurr
General Secretary
NCCB/USCC

These essays were originally prepared for the Vallombrosa meeting. The text and citations were submitted by the participants and reprinted—with a few exceptions—in their entirety.

Cover art: Artville, LLC, copyright © 1997. Used with permission.

First Printing, February 2000

ISBN 1-57455-356-9

# Contents

# Participants

CONGREGATION FOR THE DOCTRINE OF THE FAITH
His Eminence Joseph Cardinal Ratzinger, Prefect
Most Reverend Tarcisio Bertone, Secretary
Reverend Adriano Garuti, OFM, Head of Doctrinal Section
Reverend Monsignor Josef Clemens, staff
Reverend Charles Brown, staff

NATIONAL CONFERENCE OF CATHOLIC BISHOPS (USA)
Most Reverend Daniel E. Pilarczyk, Archbishop of Cincinnati
Most Reverend William J. Levada, Archbishop of San Francisco
Very Reverend J. Augustine Di Noia, OP, staff

CANADIAN CONFERENCE OF CATHOLIC BISHOPS
His Eminence Aloysius Cardinal Ambrozic,
Archbishop of Toronto
Reverend Gilles Langevin, SJ, staff

NEW ZEALAND CATHOLIC BISHOPS' CONFERENCE
Most Reverend Peter J. Cullinane, Bishop of Palmerston North

AUSTRALIAN CATHOLIC BISHOPS' CONFERENCE
Most Reverend Eric D'Arcy, Archbishop of Hobart
Most Reverend David Walker, Bishop of Broken Bay
Most Reverend Michael Putney, Auxiliary Bishop of Brisbane

CATHOLIC BISHOPS' CONFERENCE OF PAPUA NEW GUINEA AND
SOLOMON ISLANDS
Most Reverend Adrian Smith, Archbishop of Honiara
Most Reverend Gérard-Joseph Deschamps,
Bishop of Daru-Kiunga

CEPAC—EPISCOPAL CONFERENCE OF THE PACIFIC
Most Reverend Michel Marie Calvet, Archbishop of Nouméa
Most Reverend Soane Foliaki, Bishop of Tonga

# Conclusions of Doctrinal Commissions Meeting

❧❧❧

## VALLOMBROSA CENTER, MENLO PARK, CALIF.
## FEBRUARY 9-12, 1999

## I. General Description of the Meeting

From February 9 to 12, 1999, a meeting at Vallombrosa Center in Menlo Park, Calif., brought a delegation from the Congregation for the Doctrine of the Faith (CDF) together with the Chairmen and members of the Doctrinal Commissions and/or Conference Presidents or their representatives from North America and Oceania. Discussions during the meeting centered on various doctrinal questions related to the proclamation of the truth of Jesus Christ in the very diverse cultural circumstances represented by the participating Bishops.

Joseph Cardinal Ratzinger, Prefect, and Archbishop Tarcisio Bertone, Secretary, led the delegation from the Congregation for the Doctrine of the Faith. Representing the Episcopal Conference of the Pacific were Archbishop Michel Marie Calvet of Nouméa (New Caledonia) and Bishop Soane Foliaki of Tonga. From Papua New Guinea and Solomon Islands came Archbishop Adrian Smith of Honiara and Bishop Gérard-Joseph Deschamps of Daru-Kiunga. New Zealand was represented by Bishop Peter J. Cullinane of Palmerston North, and Australia by Archbishop Eric D'Arcy of Hobart, Bishop David Walker of Broken Bay, and Auxiliary Bishop Michael Putney of Brisbane. Aloysius Cardinal Ambrozic, Archbishop of Toronto, represented the Canadian Bishops' Conference, and Archbishop Daniel E. Pilarczyk of Cincinnati joined Archbishop William J. Levada of San Francisco in representing the United States. The Bishops were assisted by Congregation Officials; Reverend Adriano Garuti, OFM, Head of the Doctrinal Section; Msgr. Josef Clemens; and Reverend Charles Brown; as well as by Reverend Gilles Langevin, SJ, and Very Reverend J. Augustine Di Noia, OP, staff to the Canadian and U.S. Doctrinal Commissions, respectively.

As expressions of *affectus collegialis,* the Congregation for the Doctrine of the Faith sponsored a series of meetings with representatives of Doctrinal Commissions in regions throughout the world. Similar gatherings have been held in Latin America (Bogotá, 1984, and Guadalajara, 1996), Africa (Kinshasa, 1987), Europe (Vienna, 1989), and Asia (Hong Kong, 1993). As in previous joint meetings, the Vallombrosa meeting focused in part on the way in which doctrinal unity expresses and fosters ecclesial communion in both the local Church and the Universal Church, and at the same time contributes to a vigorous witness to the faith in diverse cultures. At Vallombrosa, the participating Bishops reported on the doctrinal situation in their particular regions as well as on the ways in which effective collaboration between Doctrinal Commissions and the Congregation for the Doctrine of the Faith might be enhanced. Extended discussion centered on topics such as the authority of the Church's Magisterium, the importance of the Profession of Faith, the ecclesial role of the theologian, and dialogue between Bishops and theologians. Other issues receiving attention at the meeting were the implications of feminism for Catholic thought and the pastoral care of homosexual persons.

Cardinal Ratzinger opened the four-day meeting with a presentation on the theme of "Subjectivity, Christology, and the Church," in which he discussed the challenges which the modern relativistic culture poses for Christian proclamation of the truth of the person of Jesus Christ as well as the uniqueness of the Church in the salvific plan of God. In referring to the question of the unity of Catholic teaching in the multiplicity of human cultures, the Cardinal stated that because the Word of God is "prior to human speech," all cultures can receive the truth about the person of Christ and every human language "can become the bearer of God's Word."

Archbishop Bertone developed a similar theme at the meeting in his presentation on "The Magisterium of the Church and the *Professio Fidei*." He stressed that obedience to the truth of Jesus Christ represents "not a suppression of the intellect," but "a progressive harmonization of one's mind and heart with the mind and heart of God." Archbishop Bertone reviewed recent magisterial documents in order to clarify the nature of the infallibility enjoyed by the ordinary and universal Magisterium as well as to reflect on the problems posed by public dissent and on possible means to remedy these problems.

In his presentation on "The Role of the Theologian in a Catholic College or University in the Light of *Ad Tuendam Fidem* and the *Professio Fidei*," Archbishop Pilarczyk stressed that theology arises out of faith and responds to this divine gift by seeking to understand and interpret Catholic doctrine in communion with the Magisterium. He asserted that the "close affinity between theologians and the hierarchical Magisterium" is based on their common concern "with understanding divine truth in human language."

"Collaboration between the Congregation for the Doctrine of the Faith and Doctrinal Commissions of Episcopal Conferences" was the title of Reverend Garuti's presentation. He commented on the relevance of the Congregation's circular letter on Doctrinal Commissions (1990) and the recent apostolic letter *Apostolos Suos* (1998) for understanding the nature and functions of Doctrinal Commissions. "While noting the fundamental difference with regard to the exercise of jurisdiction," he said, "it must be noted that there are similarities in structure and purpose between Doctrinal Commissions and the Congregation for the Doctrine of the Faith." Reverend Garuti's presentation contained many practical suggestions for ways in which the Doctrinal Commissions might collaborate with the Congregation for the Doctrine of the Faith in promoting and defending Catholic doctrine. Some of these proposals are incorporated in the third section of this document.

In addressing "The Implications of Feminism for Catholic Doctrine," Cardinal Ambrozic asserted that "women could not find an ally more clearly determined than the Church to recognize and defend their dignity." In this light, Cardinal Ambrozic was able to sketch some broad areas of agreement between certain feminist ideas and the teaching of the Church. At the same time, he identified three possible areas of divergence: "the ontological significance of the difference between the sexes, the originality and historicity of Christianity, and the value of the symbolic or sacramental dimension of the body and sexuality." Cardinal Ambrozic insisted that the universal call to holiness is addressed to women and men equally, and has primacy "over every structure and every distinction in the Church of Christ."

Archbishop D'Arcy, in his presentation on "The Problem of Homosexuality: Doctrinal Issues and Pastoral Implications," stressed the holistic way in which the Church approaches the biblical teaching on human sexuality and on homosexuality. He distinguished this Catholic approach from "proof-texting," which seeks to ground Christian teaching on homosexuality on a few passages of Sacred Scripture. Echoing a theme sounded by Cardinal Ratzinger in his opening address, Archbishop D'Arcy reiterated the Catholic rejection of the moral relativism that denies the objectivity of moral truth and moral reality. The meeting reiterated the Church's teaching, based upon Scripture and sound moral reasoning, that homosexual acts cannot contribute to the authentic good of the human person. At the same time, the importance of appropriate pastoral care for homosexual persons was emphasized, together with the Church's consistent condemnation of violence against homosexual persons.

These prepared papers were followed by a series of presentations in which participating Bishops reported on the doctrinal situation in their regions: Archbishop Smith for the Catholic Bishops' Conference of Papua New Guinea and Solomon Islands; Bishop Foliaki for the Episcopal Conference of the Pacific; Bishop Putney for the Australian Catholic Bishops' Conference; Bishop Cullinane for the New Zealand Catholic Bishops' Conference; Archbishop Levada for the National Conference of Catholic Bishops of the United States; and Cardinal Ambrozic for the Canadian Conference of Catholic Bishops. A summary of some of the main themes of these presentations follows.

## II. THEMES OF CONSENSUS

From the presentations of the various representatives concerning the doctrinal situation in their particular regions, some points of consensus emerged:

1. Cultural pluralism is profoundly present, although taking different forms, throughout the areas represented. The Bishops agreed that the encyclical letter *Fides et Ratio* (no. 5) of Pope John Paul II gives a precise and most helpful analysis of this situation. In a cultural situation of "undifferentiated pluralism," Christians cannot accept uncritically the presuppositions and values of the dominant culture. In this context, more effective doctrinal formation is very important. A new evangelization is urgently required, even within the Church. The current difficulties—even the crisis—faced by the mainstream Christian communities, as well as the aggressivity of proselytizing sects, reinforces the sense of urgency for a renewed commitment within the Church to authentic Catholic doctrine and to the sense of belonging to the Church. In such a context, it is important that doctrinal dissent, which often forms alliances with elements of secular culture in disparaging the Church's message and teaching, be forcefully and charitably answered.

2.  The assembled Bishops expressed deep gratitude for the *Catechism of the Catholic Church* and explained the ways in which it is used in their regions for education in the Catholic faith.

3.  Developments in medical techniques pose many urgent and important questions for the Church in the area of bioethics. It was noted that the *Ethical and Religious Directives for Catholic Health Care Services* of the National Conference of Catholic Bishops (USA) could be an important resource for other Conferences. Furthermore, the representatives noted the presence, throughout the regions, of many pastoral initiatives relating to family life and pro-life issues. What is needed as well is a renewed and deepened understanding of Christian anthropology to provide the adequate foundation for the proclamation and comprehension of the Church's teaching in these areas, including the question of homosexuality. With regard for the role of women in society and the Church, it was agreed that the Church should commit herself to vigorous action against all forms of violence and abuse of women. Furthermore, the theology of the nuptial significance of the human body and the corresponding notion of the complementarity of the sexes—crucial elements of the Church's understanding of the relationship between men and women in Christ—need further theological development. Reflection on the baptismal call to sanctity must be deepened, as well as the proper sense of the ordained ministry as sacrificial service and not as domination; in this way, the Church will be able to preach more convincingly the truth that "the greatest in the Kingdom of heaven are not the ministers, but the saints" (CDF, *Inter Insigniores*, p. 6).

4.  The artificiality, for the Christian, of the separation between faith and morality was discussed by the participants. The division between doctrine and moral life is seen as a serious problem. It is necessary therefore to recreate unity and coherence between theory and life, between Church teaching and practice. Doctrine

cannot be detached from life; indeed, the faithful living of the moral life is a primary form of witness and evangelization.

5.  In the resolution of doctrinal and moral questions, as well as in other areas, the importance of the role of Catholic theologians in the life of the Church and in effective collaboration with the hierarchy was noted. In the area of Catholic education, for example, it is critical that those who will teach as catechists have received adequate doctrinal formation. The importance of theologians in the Church should not be underestimated; theirs is the important and demanding task of thinking with the Church (*sentire cum Ecclesia*). From this follows the importance of recovering and of promoting the correct mutual relationship between theologians and the Magisterium, as well as the importance of the juridical expression of the relationship of communion, as given in the *Code of Canon Law* and the apostolic constitution of Pope John Paul II *Ex Corde Ecclesiae*. The theologian exists in the heart of the Church and it is there that he exercises his specific ecclesial vocation.

6.  The Catholic theologian, like all members of the Catholic faithful, receives revelation and grace through the mediation of the Church.

## III. CONCRETE PROPOSALS

The common responsibilities of the Congregation for the Doctrine of the Faith and Doctrinal Commissions derive from their respective functions. The Congregation for the Doctrine of the Faith is that body of the Apostolic See with "the function of promoting and safeguarding doctrine on faith and morals throughout the Catholic world" (cf. *Pastor Bonus*, no. 48). "In accomplishing this purpose, it renders a service to the truth, by protecting the right of the People of God to receive the Gospel message in its purity and entirety" (CDF, *Ratio Agendi*, no. 1). In an analogous way, the Doctrinal

Commissions serve Episcopal Conferences and individual Bishops in promoting and defending the Catholic faith. The following are some practical proposals which emerged from the meeting:

1.  It is the Bishops who have the primary task as teachers of the Catholic faith. They proclaim the Gospel of salvation and see to it that the faith of their people grows and deepens. It must be emphasized, therefore, that Doctrinal Commissions, while established by the various Conferences of Bishops and at the service of the Conference as such, must also make themselves directly available to the needs of individual Bishops.

2.  In certain geographical areas, the formation of joint Doctrinal Commissions serving two or more Episcopal Conferences should be seriously considered.

3.  With regard to membership in Doctrinal Commissions, it should be noted that only Bishops and those who are equivalent to Bishops in canon law can be full members.

4.  The Doctrinal Commissions should make use of the documents issued by the Holy See, especially those published by the Congregation for the Doctrine of the Faith. These documents can be distributed, reprinted, commented upon, and adapted to local needs by the Doctrinal Commissions. In particular, efforts should be made to translate and distribute the series of volumes published by the Congregation entitled *Documenti e Studi*.

5.  In order to ensure the exchange of information regarding the life and teaching of the Church, it would be important to evaluate and to enhance communication and coordination on all levels— whether between dioceses, within the structures of the Episcopal Conferences, among various Conferences of Bishops, and with the Congregation for the Doctrine of the Faith.

6. Doctrinal Commissions should send their publications and, depending on the nature of the documents, those of other Commissions as well to the Congregation for the Doctrine of the Faith on an annual basis.

7. It is strongly recommended that every Doctrinal Commission send an annual report on the doctrinal situation of its region to the Congregation for the Doctrine of the Faith. The report should mention areas of ongoing study, particular doctrinal problems, the situation in centers of ministerial formation, and other questions. Suggestions can also be included regarding the best way that the Holy See might address local doctrinal questions. On its part, the Congregation for the Doctrine of the Faith should periodically send the Doctrinal Commissions information regarding its activities. Periodic meetings between the Congregation for the Doctrine of the Faith and Doctrinal Commissions are very helpful; these can take place in Rome or in the areas of the different Episcopal Conferences.

8. The Doctrinal Commission should prepare a special report for submission to the Congregation for the Doctrine of the Faith on the occasion of the *ad limina* visit of the members of the Bishops' Conferences.

9. Collaboration between the Congregation for the Doctrine of the Faith and the Doctrinal Commissions becomes particularly relevant with respect to the examination of publications presenting doctrinal problems. In this matter, the responsibility of the first instance belongs with the local Ordinary who may seek the assistance of the Doctrinal Commission. Later, if necessary, an intervention on the part of the Congregation for the Doctrine of the Faith may be requested. However, the Congregation may intervene on its own if the gravity of the case demands it, or whenever a doctrinal problem goes beyond the territorial boundaries

of a particular Conference. In any case, the situation will be resolved in close collaboration with the local Ordinary.

10. Doctrinal Commissions should be available to assist local Bishops in the work of evaluating books and other publications which have been submitted for the *imprimatur*. They can also draw up lists of theological experts, which can be provided to individual Bishops for collaboration in this area.

11. The Doctrinal Commission can also be of assistance to local Bishops when, as required by canon law, a theologian requests the *mandatum* from a competent ecclesiastical authority in order to teach theology in a Catholic college or university.

12. The Doctrinal Commission should be consulted by the other Commissions of the Conferences of Bishops in the process of drafting any documents for publication which have doctrinal aspects or implications. This includes, in a special way, ecumenical agreements. The other Commissions of the Conference should not publish important documents without first having received the judgment of the Doctrinal Commission in what pertains to its competence.


## IV. FINAL CONCLUSION

The assembled Bishops will report to their respective Episcopal Conferences regarding the work of the meeting and the conclusions reached.

# Congregation for the Doctrine of the Faith

# *DEUS LOCUTUS EST NOBIS IN FILIO*: SOME REFLECTIONS ON SUBJECTIVITY, CHRISTOLOGY, AND THE CHURCH

⚜

HIS EMINENCE
JOSEPH CARDINAL RATZINGER

## I. THE CULTURAL AND THEOLOGICAL CONTEXT

In seeking to sum up the situation of Catholic theology as we come to the end of this century—and indeed to the end of the millennium—more than one observer has remarked that the twentieth century can be divided into two periods: an initial period of intense and fruitful development, almost unparalleled in the history of the Church, which culminated in the Second Vatican Council; and a subsequent period of dissipation in which the earlier accomplishments have not continued. Perhaps there is a certain inevitability in such a process. Recently, in assessing the current state of theology, Christoph Cardinal Schönborn chose to use a phrase which had been coined by another Archbishop of Vienna, Cardinal König, who, when asked about theology today, responded that what we have is "*molta teologia—poco Dio*": a lot of theology but little about God.[1] In a certain sense, this phrase—with the contradiction it expresses—captures the present situation fairly well. There is more "theologizing" than ever, but it seems that increasingly little of it dares to speak about God.

The roots of the current situation are, however, as much philosophical as they are theological. We find ourselves at the end of the century in a cultural situation characterized by what might be called a "one-sided concern to investigate human subjectivity."[2] Certainly, the importance of subjectivity cannot be disregarded or minimized. In fact, one of the great accomplishments of theology in the decades leading up to the Second Vatican Council was its concern to show that Catholic doctrine was not simply an elaborate impersonal "system" of truths, but rather a call to the fulfillment of the authentic dignity of the human person, because Christ, the second Adam, is the long-awaited manifestation of what it means to be truly human, the definitive revelation to man of his own human nature: "it is only in the mystery of the Word that the mystery of man truly becomes clear."[3]

Theology, however, is not practiced in a vacuum, and the cultural climate has become one in which a legitimate interest in human subjectivity has deteriorated to the point where the subject alone becomes the fundamental point of reference for all else. The paradoxical situation arises in which the various human sciences demonstrate the limitations and contingency of every subjective viewpoint, while at the same time it is the unspoken assumption that all subjective perspectives are equally valid, a view which, as the encyclical letter *Fides et Ratio* observes, "is one of today's most widespread symptoms of the lack of confidence in truth."[4] Thus, a philosophical climate has established itself which, in its exaggerated subjectivism, is highly skeptical with regard to questions of truth and meaning, believing instead that there is nothing more than various and competing interpretations. It is a subjectivism which is not limited to a cultural elite, but is found diffused throughout society and takes the characteristic form of a pervasive relativism.

It is significant too that, within philosophy, a unilateral focus on human subjectivity has led to a decline of interest in metaphysics and a corresponding increase in the investigation of the phenomenon of language, linguistics, and hermeneutics. In such fields, it is not unusual to hear the argument that language is essentially self-referential, that there is no point in speaking about a reality beyond language, or in speaking about truth.[5] At the same time, political critiques of language seek to show how "meanings" are created and maintained in order to preserve power and perpetuate social forms. The encyclical letter *Fides et Ratio* speaks of a "crisis of meaning"[6] which sums up the situation quite well, insofar as the question for modern man has become not "are the claims of the Christian religion true?" (do they correspond to what is real?), but rather "is there any reality beyond our interpretations?" It is remarkable also how much contemporary interest there is within theology on questions of language and hermeneutics; it is in this sense that Cardinal König's remark is true.

Undoubtedly, part of the reason for the contemporary dominance of relativism is that it would seem that this perspective has had impressive results when applied to the area of political or civil life. Relativism presents itself on the political plane in the form of pluralism, as the basis for a democratic system of government, which is founded precisely on the fact that, in matters of social policy, there can certainly be a diversity of legitimate options, and thus no single vision can claim to be absolute. In a democracy, the different perspectives recognize the others as partial tendencies for achieving what is best and seek to form a consensus through dialogue and compromise. Political freedom requires a system in which relative positions communicate among themselves and remain always open to new developments. A liberal society would thus be a relativistic society, and only as such can it remain an open society, characterized by tolerance and freedom.

In the area of politics, this manner of thinking is correct up to a certain point. It is true that no political option can define itself as the only correct one. What is relative cannot be made absolute—to believe the contrary is precisely the error of totalitarian political ideologies. However, experience also shows that, when the constituents of a political democracy lack an adequate appreciation for the objective good of the human person, the mere presence of a democratic system is not sufficient to prevent serious evils. Injustices do not become just simply because they have become the consensus of the majority (e.g., the killing of the innocent, institutionalized racism, or wars of aggression). Thus, even in the political realm, relativism must impose limits on itself, and those limits are to be found in the irrevocable requirements of a truth about man which transcends the subjectivity of the human person. Today, in the absence of a common commitment to fundamental human goods, democratic societies seem to be becoming increasingly polarized and legitimate consensus harder to obtain. What this shows is that a one-sided emphasis on subjectivity tends toward increasing fragmentation and isolation within human society.

When relativism is explicitly adopted in the areas of faith and morals, the consequences are grave. In the area of moral theology, the phenomenon is well-known and does not require much comment. It is manifested most characteristically in the view which would attribute to the individual conscience the ability to make infallible decisions about good and evil, the notion that a "moral judgment is true merely by the fact that it has its origin in the conscience."[7] As the encyclical letter *Veritatis Splendor* correctly points out, "such an outlook is quite congenial to an individualistic ethic, wherein each individual is faced with his own truth, different from the truth of others."[8] If, in philosophy and the human sciences, the investigation into human subjectivity paradoxically illustrates the limitations of the human subject (indeed, the manner in which he may even be determined culturally), while also presuming that there is no viewpoint beyond the subjective, an analogous dynamic presents itself in moral theology in the simultaneous exaltation of human freedom and radical questioning about whether men are indeed truly free.

Even in popular approaches to theology, one finds similar patterns of thought among some Catholic theologians. Perhaps the most common approach is that which begins by maintaining that the reality named by the word "God" is completely beyond our understanding; that is, an uncritical and exaggerated apophaticism is posited. Next, the function of theology becomes understood as that of interpreting or reinterpreting the "foundational texts" of a particular community, texts which are viewed as the expression of that community's notion or experience of God. The final step is taken when this task of reinterpretation is then exercised at the service of some program; one thinks of certain forms of liberation theology or, more recently, of the hermeneutic employed by some feminist theologians. Notwithstanding the evident intelligence of some of the practitioners of these models of interpretative theology, what often emerges from such work is a tedious predictability. The results are almost always totally foreseeable; it is as if the solution were pre-ordained—as in a sense it is. One finds in such attempts a repetition of what George Tyrrell humorously criticized in the work of Adolf Harnack: "the Christ that Harnack sees, looking back through nineteen centuries of Catholic darkness, is only the reflection of a Liberal Protestant face, seen at the bottom of a deep well."[9]

One also sees elements of the same phenomenon in what has been called the theology of religious pluralism, which in some parts of the world seems to be assuming the place which a decade ago was occupied by liberation theology. Its configurations are quite different, but what is interesting are its essential lines, above all with regard to the question of truth. The theology of religious pluralism is, on one side, the product of the Western world and its post-Enlightenment philosophical conceptions; on the other, it makes use of the philosophical and religious intuitions of Asia, and it is precisely the connection between these two worlds that determines its particular influence at the present historical moment.

The theology of Christian pluralism is shaped by its Kantian philosophical presuppositions; it is assumed that God, or Ultimate reality, is transcendent and inaccessible, and thus can be experienced only through images and ideas that are culturally conditioned. Thus, what is perceived by the human subject is not reality as it is, but only its representation through our particular system of perception. These epistemological presuppositions are then applied to Christology, and it is asserted that the identification of a single historical figure, Jesus of Nazareth, with the reality of God himself is a form of mythological thinking, true only in the sense that it may be helpful for believers to think in this way. The person of Jesus is expressly relativized so as to become one of a variety of religious masters. History presents us with many such models, ideal figures, who refer us back to what is ultimately real, to the Absolute, the divine mystery which is totally beyond human thought and history.

From this christological position follows a necessary reduction in the understanding of the Church, of doctrine, and of sacraments. They are not formally abandoned because, on the contrary, they serve an important symbolic role in directing our attention to the divine, to that which transcends history. But to attribute to these means an absolute character, even as derived from and based upon the absolute event of Jesus Christ, would be to place what is particular on an absolute plane and to distort the infinity of God, who is always beyond what religions can perceive. Similarly, in such a perspective, to maintain that universally valid truth is found in the historical person of Jesus Christ and in the faith of the Church comes to be seen as a fundamentalism opposed to the spirit of modernity and as a threat to the principal goods of tolerance and freedom.

Furthermore, it is maintained that only through the acceptance of such a relativism can there be authentic dialogue and tolerance. Entering into dialogue would signify exactly what it signifies in the model of political pluralism: the recognition that all perspectives are equally true. Thus, the process of dialogue tends to become a substitute for the search for truth itself. But this is something far different from what was understood in the patristic and scholastic tradition, as well as in the Second Vatican Council. In reality, dialogue comes into being when there is not only speaking but also listening, a listening which becomes the basis of an encounter that leads to reciprocal comprehension. But as St. Augustine recognized in his own experience of dialogue, human beings are capable of true mutual understanding only when they are conscious of communicating in the truth: the greater their commitment to the fundamental reality of truth, the greater will be their capacity to discover real common ground. Thus, a theological perspective which prefers to set aside the question of truth as something not essential to the discussion, or as even counterproductive, is not really able to enter into authentic dialogue. "To believe it is possible to know a universally valid truth is in no way to encourage intolerance; on the contrary, it is the essential condition for sincere and authentic dialogue between persons."[10]

## II. THE UNIQUENESS OF THE PERSON OF JESUS CHRIST

As this brief survey has pointed out, in the cultural context of subjectivism and increasing relativism, it is the very notion of revelation that becomes viewed as problematic, and with this comes a corresponding reduction in the understanding of the person of Christ. We find ourselves in a situation in which some theologians, both within and without the Catholic Church, have become uncomfortable with what seems to be the exclusivistic implications of asserting that in the historical person of Jesus Christ, God himself has become a human being and has spoken to us.

In other words, in a philosophical climate which has become highly skeptical with regard to the question of truth and meaning, and which tends to believe that all we can offer are various and competing systems of interpretations and symbols, it comes to be viewed as useless to speak of something true or real which stands behind these interpretations. In such a climate, the person of Christ tends to be viewed in theology increasingly as a symbol and correspondingly less as a person. This "symbolization" of the person of Christ can take various forms: it can take a relatively conservative form in which Christ is seen as the definitive symbol of the human need for God; it can take the form of seeing Christ as a symbol of the struggle for liberation from unjust social structures or from the oppression of a patriarchal society. But every symbolization of the person of Christ presupposes that there can be other ways, other symbols, for expressing what Christ symbolizes. Christ is a symbol, an expression of God—even a privileged symbol—but it is recognized that there can be other symbols. The most important consequence of this conception is that Jesus Christ cannot be considered the unique, exclusive mediator. Only for Christians is he the human form of God, the one who facilitates man's encounter with God.[11]

In the face of these perspectives, it is critical that theology recover an authentic sense of the person of Jesus Christ, because in the final analysis *only a person can be something more than a symbol*; a person is someone who speaks to us, who speaks a word to us which we receive in faith. There is a great difference between the attitude which seeks to listen to a person who speaks a word and the attitude which seeks to interpret a symbol. It is the difference between receiving meaning and creating meaning, between understanding and self-assertion.

Indeed, the central claim of the Christian faith is the fact that through a completely free decision, God has decided to reveal himself and to give himself to man. This revelation has its definitive and final culmination in the person of the Incarnate Word, "himself both the mediator and the sum total of revelation."[12] As the author of the Letter to the Hebrews writes, "In these last days [God] has spoken to us by a Son."[13] The *Catechism of the Catholic Church* appropriately includes, as a kind of commentary on this passage, the words of St. John of the Cross: "In giving us his Son, his only Word (for he possesses no other), he spoke everything to us at once in this sole Word."[14] It is significant that the *Catechism* chooses John of the Cross to help explain what revelation means; in this we are reminded that theology has its origin in the encounter with a Word that is always prior to us, a Word who is a person. Theology begins in the receptiveness of faith, and it is for this reason that the saints are theologians in the fullest sense of the term.

In this connection, I would note that in the period since the last meeting, in 1996, between the Congregation for the Doctrine of the Faith and Doctrinal Commissions of Episcopal Conferences, there have been several important steps taken by the Holy See with regard to Catholic doctrine. I have already referred to the encyclical *Fides et Ratio*; later in our meeting we will speak about others: the apostolic letter *Ad Tuendam Fidem* and accompanying commentary on the *Professio Fidei*, and also the apostolic letter *Apostolos Suos*. But there has been another development of significance for Catholic theology which perhaps does not come immediately to mind, and that is the declaration of St. Thérèse of the Child Jesus as a Doctor of the Church. In a certain sense, the decision of the Holy Father to declare formally the "eminent doctrine" of this saint is an important and timely reminder of what theology ought to be; the Pope expresses this with succinctness in his apostolic letter *Divini Amoris Scientia*: "As it was for the Church's saints in every age, so also for her; in her spiritual experience Christ is the centre and fullness of revelation. Thérèse knew Jesus, loved him and made him loved with the passion of a bride."[15] To know the person of Christ—this is the foundation of theology.

In the final analysis, the Church's claim that Jesus of Nazareth is the center and fullness of revelation, the only mediator between God and the human race, in whom all truth is found, is simply her articulation of the response of faith to the person who has revealed himself to her. It is the conviction, as St. Paul confesses, that the "obedience of faith" must be given to God as he reveals himself.[16] The Church ultimately is made up of those who believe that this Word is true; it is in this sense that she is the spouse of the Word; she listens to the Word and is formed by the Word. Indeed, it is in the liturgy of the Church that this listening is continually accomplished.

But the fact of the radical uniqueness of the person of Jesus Christ, the fact that he is the Word of God spoken to humanity, does not—contrary to what some would assert—imply the destruction or homogenization of human cultures. In fact, it is precisely the opposite. All cultures can receive this Word precisely because it is a Word which is prior to human speech. This truth is recalled by the Holy Father in *Fides et Ratio* in connection with the listing of peoples in the Pentecost account of the Acts of the Apostles,[17] which narrates how *through all languages and in all languages,* that is, in all cultures which manifest themselves in language, the testimony about Jesus Christ becomes understandable. In all of them, the human word becomes the bearer of God's own language, of God's own *Logos.* The encyclical puts it this way: "While it demands of all who hear it the adherence of faith, the proclamation of the Gospel in different cultures allows people to preserve their own cultural identity. This in no way creates division, because the community of the baptized is marked by a universality which can embrace every culture."[18]

It is by the receptivity of faith in the concrete person of Jesus Christ, through the Spirit, that an authentic pluralism can develop: pluralism happens not when it is made the explicit object of our desire, but when one seeks to receive the truth with all its power. To desire to receive the person of Christ in faith requires that, instead of making myself the measure, I have the trust to accept as the voice and the way of truth the greater understanding which is present as a prior given in the Church's faith.

## III. THE SUBJECT OF THE CHURCH AND THE MEANING OF THE PHRASE *SUBSISTIT IN*

That the Church is the community brought into being by the faithful reception of this single and definitive Word of God implies that it will become a community shaped by the common receptivity to this Word, a common listening which takes place not only at a single moment of history, but a listening which transcends history. Empirically speaking, it was the preaching of the apostles in different languages and cultural contexts which called into existence the social organization of the Church as a kind of single historical subject. One becomes a believer by joining this community of tradition, thought and life, by living personally from its continuity of life throughout history, and by acquiring a share in its way of understanding, its speech and its thought. For the believer, however, the Church is not a sociological subject created by human agreement, but a truly new subject called into being by the Word and in the Holy Spirit; and pre-cisely for that reason, the Church herself overcomes the seemingly insurmountable confines of human subjectivity by putting man in contact with the ground of reality which is prior to him.

The Church can be so identified with Christ that she can be called his "body." This bodily unity is to be understood against the biblical con-cept of man and wife: they are to become two in one flesh.[19] It is a unity created through the unifying power of love, which does not destroy the duality of the two but unites them in a profound oneness. And it is here that we find the answer to the problem of human sub-jectivity mentioned above; it is here that the poles of human subjec-tivity and the uniqueness of the person of Christ are resolved in the concrete subject of the Church. It is in Christ that the Christian finds his own identity as a subject; in being identified with Christ, in being one with him, one's own self is restored. In the experience of faith, the Christian knows that he has been accepted by Christ and he is thus enabled to give himself freely to Christ. In this process, the human subject becomes an embodiment of the Church; he simultaneously finds his identity and experiences the purification of human subjectivity, a surrendering of the self and a being drawn into the innermost nature of what is meant by the word "Church." The Christian's inclusion in this single ecclesial subject finds paramount expression liturgically as a single response of faith, a response *in persona ecclesiae*, to God's revelation when we together say: "I believe." By its very nature, faith is this believing communion with the whole Church. The "I believe" of the Creed refers not to some private "I," but rather to the corporate "I" of the Church.

It has always been the conviction of the Church that her subjectivity possesses a recognizable delineation; she is one in faith, one in the celebration of the sacraments, one in apostolic succession, and one in ecclesial governance. The Second Vatican Council teaches the historical continuity between the Church founded by Christ and the Catholic Church in the now-famous paragraph 8 of *Lumen Gentium*: "This Church, constituted and organized as a society in the present world, subsists in the Catholic Church, governed by the Successor of Peter and by the Bishops in communion with him, although outside of her structure, many elements can be found of sanctification and truth which, as gifts properly belonging to the Church of Christ, impel toward Catholic unity."[20]

As the response of the House of Bishops of the Church of England to the Encyclical *Ut Unum Sint* noted, the phrase *subsistit in* has been interpreted "in different ways both within the Catholic Church and elsewhere."[21] In 1985, the Congregation for the Doctrine of the Faith sought to clarify somewhat the mistaken interpretations of the phrase *subsistit in*, by declaring that Leonardo Boff's understanding of subsistence, in which the Church of Christ "may also be present in other Christian churches," was precisely the opposite of the authentic meaning of the conciliar text.[22]

The Congregation's declaration saw a form of ecclesiological relativism in Boff's interpretation of the teaching of the Second Vatican

Council, which contradicts the Council's fundamental approach. As this relativism possesses its own logic within his ecclesiology, and since it also corresponds to a trend relatively widespread in contemporary theology, it may be helpful to examine it a bit more closely. Boff follows the exegetical theory which holds that the "historical Jesus" did not envisage a Church; the Church originated only after the resurrection in the process of de-eschatologization, due to the inevitable need for institutionalization. In this process, the Church conformed to worldly patterns and adopted a Roman and feudal style (two historical realities which, in fact, are quite distinct from each other). If this were so—that is, if the Church as an institution were due only to the process of de-eschatologization, to a moving away from Jesus' original message and to the sociological inevitability of the community's institutionalization—then all institutions within the Church would be only human works. Following from such presuppositions, Boff's conclusion—that there needs to be permanent change within the Church and that today a totally new Church is called for—is quite logical. It would also follow that there is really no concrete "Church of God"; indeed, from this viewpoint, one would have to ask whether the notion of a Church "of God" would not in fact be completely untenable. If the Church as such resulted only from the loss of the original eschatological tension and from sociological needs, then all the historical Churches are simply human constructions, having their origin in particular historical conditions and, under certain circumstances, must be capable of radical modification. At the most, the Churches would differ from one another only secondarily in their theological quality, but Boff assumes that the "one Church of Christ" could "subsist" in many Churches.

The starting point for Catholic (and Orthodox) theology is, however, quite different. It is clear that the foundation of the Church cannot be ascribed to a hypothetically constructed "historical Jesus," since, from this point of departure, the idea of the Church has no place. Catholic tradition, however, as already mentioned, chooses a different starting point: *it trusts the evangelists and believes them.* Thus, it becomes clear that Jesus, who announced the kingdom of God, also gathered disciples around him for its realization. He did not only give them his word as a new interpretation of the Old Testament but also, in the Sacrament of the Last Supper, bestowed on them a new unifying center, through which all those who confess faith in him become one with him in a totally new way, in a unity so profound that St. Paul could describe the community as a being-one-body with Christ, a spiritual body-unity. Thus, it also becomes clear that the promise of the Holy Spirit is not just a vague announcement, but refers to the reality of Pentecost, to the fact that the Church is not thought up and produced by man but is created by the Spirit; the Church is and always remains the work of the Holy Spirit.

Therefore, the relationship in the Church between institution and Spirit is different from what Boff, and with him some other modern theologians, would propose. The institution is not something that can be deconstructed and reconstructed at will, something that has nothing to do with the reality of faith as such. Rather, this form of bodiliness belongs to the Church herself. The Church of Christ is not something intangible, hidden under the variety of human constructions, but she truly exists as a bodily Church, identified through the confession of faith, the sacraments, and apostolic succession. It is significant that in his recent *Dogmengeschichte*, the Lutheran theologian Wolfgang Bienert departs decisively from Harnack and the liberal positions widely held in the first half of the twentieth century.[23] He argues instead that the three "pre-dogmatic fundamental norms" (as he calls them), "the confession of faith as the norm of truth," the Biblical canon, and the ecclesial (or episcopal ministry)—elements which are commonly referred to as "early Catholicism"—are not a break from the origin, but profoundly correspond to it and serve its realization.

But "ecclesiological relativism" must also be considered from another angle. If the Church only "subsists" intangibly under the various "Churches," then no Church could claim to possess definitively binding teaching authority, and in this way institutional relativism will lead to doctrinal relativism. If belief in "the body" of the Church is taken away, the Church's concrete claims regarding the content of the faith disappear along with her bodiliness.

What the Second Vatican Council wished to express with the *subsistit* formula—in complete fidelity to the Catholic tradition—is precisely the opposite of any "ecclesiological relativism." It is that *the Church of Jesus Christ exists.* Christ himself has willed her existence; and since Pentecost, the Holy Spirit continuously creates her and, despite every human failure, preserves the Church in her essential identity. The institution is not an inevitable yet theologically irrelevant or even detrimental formality, but rather, in its essential nucleus, belongs to the concreteness of the incarnation. The Lord keeps his word: "The gates of hell shall not prevail against it."[24]

At this point, it is important to examine the word *subsistit* a bit more closely. With this term, the Council explicated the formula of Pope Pius XII, who had stated in his encyclical letter *Mystici Corporis Christi* that the Catholic Church "is" *(est)* the one mystical body of Christ. In the distinction between *subsistit* and *est* is hidden the entire ecumenical problem. The word *subsistit* derives from ancient philosophy, as it was later developed among the Scholastics. It corresponds to the Greek word *hypostasis,* which of course plays a key role in Christology in describing the union of divine and human natures in the one person of Christ. *Subsistere* is a special case of *esse.* It refers to existence in the form of an individual subject. That is exactly what it means here. The Council wanted to say that the Church of Jesus Christ, as a concrete subject in the world, is found in the Catholic Church. This can only occur in a single instance, and thus the notion that *subsistit* could be multiplied precisely misses the meaning of the term. With the word *subsistit,* the Council wanted to express the singularity and non-multiplicability of the Church of Christ, the Catholic Church: the Church exists as a single subject in the reality of history. But the difference between *subsistit* and *est* also embraces the drama of ecclesial division: for while the Church is only one and really exists, there is *being* which is from the Church's *being*—there is ecclesial reality—outside the Church. Because sin is contradiction, the difference between *subsistit* and *est* cannot, in the final analysis, be completely resolved logically.

In the paradox of the difference between the Church's uniqueness and concreteness on one hand, and the existence of ecclesial reality outside this single subject on the other, the contradiction of human sin is reflected, the contradiction of division. Such a division is something quite different from the dialectic presented by Leonardo Boff and some other theologians, in which the divisions among Christians are no longer seen as something painful and, in fact, no longer seen even as a splitting, but rather viewed as descriptive of the multiplicity of variations on a theme, in which all the variations are at the same time somehow right and somehow wrong. The view of the Council is totally different. The fact that in the Catholic Church the subsistence of the one subject of the Church is present is something which can in no way be credited to Catholics, but is rather the work of God alone, which he sustains in spite of the continual discrediting failures of the members of the Church. Therefore, they have nothing about which to boast; but rather, ashamed of their sins and at the same time filled with gratitude, they should marvel at God's faithfulness. But the effects of sin are clear to everyone: the whole world sees the spectacle of separated Christian communities opposed to one another, whose claims to the truth contradict one another, and who thus seem to frustrate the very prayer of Christ on the eve of his suffering and death. While the divisions as historical realities can be grasped by anyone, the ongoing existence of the one Church in the concrete form of the Catholic Church can only be perceived by faith.

Because the Second Vatican Council understood this paradox, it explained that ecumenism is a duty which is part of the future of the Church on her way through history. Ecumenism thus seeks to reestablish, not the unity of the Church, but rather unity among all

Christians and full communion between the Catholic Church and the Churches and ecclesial communities separated from her. At the same time, we must not forget that the lack of unity among Christians is a wound for the Catholic Church, not in the sense of being deprived of her unity, but insofar as the divisions are an obstacle in the way of the full realization of her universal vocation in history.[25]

## CONCLUSION

As the encyclical *Fides et Ratio* makes clear, we find ourselves at a moment in history in which the Church—by insisting on the existence of a truth beyond subjectivity, a truth found in the person of Jesus Christ—can render a profound service to the world of philosophy and culture. This service will be given to the extent to which Christian theology becomes conscious of its authentic nature and has the courage *to speak about God*—God who has revealed himself in the person of Jesus Christ. In this way, theology becomes true wisdom and true knowledge, *divini amoris scientia*; the wisdom of the Cross; a wisdom formed by the uniqueness, the definitiveness, and the insuperability of the person of Jesus Christ; a wisdom of love in which the Church listens to the Word and speaks that Word in her own voice.

## NOTES

1    Cf. Christoph Schönborn, "La situation actuelle de la théologie," *Aletheia* 10 (December 1996): 9.

2    John Paul II, encyclical letter *Fides et Ratio* (FR), no. 5: *Acta Apostolicae Sedis* (*AAS*) 91 (1999), 9.

3    Second Vatican Council, pastoral constitution *Gaudium et Spes*, no. 22.

4    FR, no. 5: *AAS* 91 (1999), 9.

5    Cf. ibid., 84.

6    Ibid., 81.

7    John Paul II, encyclical letter *Veritatis Splendor*, no. 32: *AAS* 85 (1993), 1159.

8    Ibid., 32.

9    George Tyrrell, *Christianity at the Cross-Roads* (London: Longmans, Green & Co., 1909), 44.

10   FR, no. 92: *AAS* 91 (1999), 78.

11   Such positions are discussed in the document of the International Theological Commission, *Christianity and the World Religions* (1997), no. 21.

12   Second Vatican Council, dogmatic constitution *Dei Verbum*, no. 2.

13   Heb 1:1-2.

14   *Catechism of the Catholic Church*, no. 65.

15   John Paul II, apostolic letter *Divini Amoris Scientia*, no. 8: *AAS* 90 (1998), 938.

16   Rom 16:26; cf. Rom 1:5; 2 Cor 10:5-6.

17   Acts 2:7-11.

18   FR, 71: *AAS* 91 (1999), 60.

19   Cf. Gen 2:24; Eph 5:30ff.; 1 Cor 6:16.

20   Second Vatican Council, dogmatic constitution *Lumen Gentium,* no. 8.

21   *May They All Be One: A Response of the House of Bishops of the Church of England to* Ut Unum Sint (London: Church House Publishing, 1997), no. 56.

22   Congregation for the Doctrine of the Faith, *Notificatio de scripto P. Leonardi Boff, OFM, "Chiesa: Carisma e Potere"* (March 11, 1985): *AAS* 77 (1985), 758.

23   Wolfgang A. Bienert, *Dogmengeschichte* (Stuttgart: Kohlhammer, 1997).

24   Mt 16:18.

25   Cf. Congregation for the Doctrine of the Faith, *Litteræ ad Catholicæ Ecclesiæ episcopos de aliquibus aspectibus Eccelsiæ prout est communio* (May 28, 1992), 17: *AAS* 85 (1993), 849.

# THE MAGISTERIUM
# OF THE CHURCH AND THE
# *PROFESSIO FIDEI*

❧

### MOST REVEREND
### TARCISIO BERTONE, SDB

## INTRODUCTION

I t is an unequivocal *datum* of the Church's Tradition that she has received from her Founder the gift of the Magisterium, the vital necessity of which has been recognized throughout the long history of theological reflection.[1]

The subjects of the Magisterium are the Episcopal College together with its head, the Bishop of Rome: the Bishop of Rome as Successor of Peter and the Bishops as "teachers and judges in matters of faith and morals" in the community of the faithful entrusted to them, for whom they act as "witnesses of divine and Catholic truth."[2] In the context of the Pope's magisterial function, the Congregation for the Doctrine of the Faith exercises a "subsidiary" task.[3]

# I. RECENT DOCTRINAL DOCUMENTS

A list, though not an exhaustive one, of recent doctrinal documents of Pope John Paul II would undoubtedly include the encyclical letters *Veritatis Splendor* (1993), on fundamental questions of the moral teaching of the Church, and *Evangelium Vitae* (1995), on the value and inviolability of human life, as well as the apostolic letter *Ordinatio Sacerdotalis* (1994), on the reservation of priestly ordination to men (together with the *Responsum Ad Dubium* on the teaching of *Ordinatio Sacerdotalis* [1995]), and the apostolic letter *Ad Tuendam Fidem* (1998), by which certain norms were inserted into the *Code of Canon Law* and the *Code of Canons of the Eastern Churches,* in order to bring the canonical legislation into conformity with what is established and prescribed by the formula of the *Professio Fidei.*

For its part, the Congregation for the Doctrine of the Faith has published instructions and letters of a doctrinal-pastoral nature to orient the formation and moral behavior of the Catholic faithful: the declaration *On Certain Questions of Sexual Ethics* (*Persona Humana*) (1975), the letter *On the Pastoral Care of Homosexual Persons* (1986), and the letter *On the Reception of the Eucharist by Divorced and Remarried Members of the Faithful* (1994).

As an authoritative synthesis of the Church's common doctrine in the areas of dogmatic theology and morality, Pope John Paul II promulgated the *Catechism of the Catholic Church* (*editio typica* 1997), in order to provide, as the apostolic constitution *Fidei Depositum* explains:

> A statement of the Church's faith and of catholic doctrine, attested to or illumined by Sacred Scripture, the Apostolic Tradition and the Church's Magisterium. I declare it to be a sure norm for teaching the faith and thus a valid and legitimate instrument for ecclesial communion. May it serve the

renewal to which the Holy Spirit ceaselessly calls the Church of God, the Body of Christ, on her pilgrimage to the undiminished light of the Kingdom! The approval and publication of the *Catechism of the Catholic Church* represents a service which the Successor of Peter wishes to offer to the Holy Catholic Church, to all the particular Churches in peace and communion with the Apostolic See of Rome: the service, that is, of supporting and confirming the faith of all the Lord Jesus' disciples (cf. *Lk* 22:32), as well as strengthening the bonds of unity in the same apostolic faith.[4]

Many other documents of a doctrinal nature have been published in recent years by various Episcopal Conferences and individual Bishops.[5] Recently, the apostolic letter *Apostolos Suos* (1998) specified the conditions for the publication of doctrinal statements by Conferences of Bishops and the magisterial authority of such documents for the Christian faithful.[6]

In the present paper, I will limit myself to a consideration of three documents of paradigmatic importance with regard to the *Professio Fidei* and the three "paragraphs" of its concluding section which differentiate three categories of truths. These documents are the encyclicals *Veritatis Splendor* and *Evangelium Vitae,* and the apostolic letter *Ordinatio Sacerdotalis*. I will not consider other magisterial documents not because they do not express the certain doctrine of the Church, but simply because these three seem to be the most important from a doctrinal standpoint.

With regard to the reaction within the Church to the publication of these documents, there has been no lack of expressions of total consensus and grateful appreciation by many Cardinals, Bishops, Episcopal Conferences, and also by numerous priests and lay people who, in letters to the Holy Father and to the Congregation for the Doctrine of the Faith, have expressed their adherence to and agreement with the doctrine set forth by the Magisterium in these texts. It should be mentioned also that the pre-publication presentation of papal documents, in special meetings at the Vatican, to the Presidents of those Episcopal Conferences that are most directly concerned with the particular topic, has been widely appreciated and has strengthened the bonds of communion between the Apostolic See and individual Bishops and Bishops' Conferences. It has also contributed to the distribution and favorable reception of these documents.

On the other hand, expressions of disagreement and dissent have been raised by some theologians and groups or associations in the Church, who have questioned the content and theological basis of the teaching of these documents, as well as their doctrinal weight and binding character. They have denied that these doctrines can be qualified as *definitive* or even as *set forth infallibly* by the Magisterium. For this reason, I would like to reflect on the principal objections raised with regard to the doctrinal weight and level of authority of these teachings of the Magisterium.

## II. CENTRAL ASPECTS OF THE DEBATE ON THE MAGISTERIUM—THE INFALLIBILITY OF THE ORDINARY AND UNIVERSAL MAGISTERIUM

From the doctrinal standpoint, and in light of the principal criticisms of the above-mentioned magisterial documents, it is important to give special attention to some key points, which, in the current theological and ecclesial climate, are obscured by confusion and ambiguity, with negative consequences for the teaching of theology and for the attitude of certain groups within the Church.

1.  In the first place, one finds the tendency to measure everything through the distinction between the *infallible* and *fallible* Magisterium.

In this way, infallibility becomes the touchstone for all questions of authority, to the point that the notion of authority comes to be substituted *de facto* by that of infallibility. Very often, the question of infallibility is confused with that of the truth of a doctrine, by assuming that infallibility is a prerequisite for the truth and irreformability of a doctrine, and thus making the truth and definitiveness of a doctrine depend upon the infallibility or lack of infallibility of a specific magisterial pronouncement. In reality, the truth and irreformability of a doctrine depend upon the *depositum fidei*, transmitted in Scripture and Tradition, while infallibility refers simply to the level of certainty of a specific act of magisterial teaching. In the criticism of recent documents of the Magisterium, it is also forgotten that the infallible character of a teaching, and the definitive and irrevocable character of the assent which is owed to such teaching, are not prerogatives pertaining only to what has been solemnly "defined" by the Roman Pontiff or an Ecumenical Council. When the Bishops in communion with the Successor of Peter dispersed throughout the world in their individual dioceses teach a doctrine to be held definitively, they enjoy the same infallibility as that of the Magisterium of the Pope *ex cathedra* or of a Council.[7] It bears repeating that in the encyclicals *Veritatis Splendor* and *Evangelium Vitae,* and in the apostolic letter *Ordinatio Sacerdotalis*, the Roman Pontiff intended, though not with a solemn form, to confirm and reaffirm doctrines which belong to the teaching of the ordinary and universal Magisterium, and which therefore are to be held definitively and irrevocably.

Furthermore, it must also be noted that, although there are different levels of authority among the teachings of the Magisterium, this does not mean that the authority of a lesser level can be considered to be on the same plane as theological opinions or that, outside the area of infallibility, the only thing that counts is argumentation and that a common certainty of the Church on doctrinal matters is impossible.

2. These considerations become very important with respect to adherence to the teaching of *Veritatis Splendor, Evangelium Vitae, Ordinatio Sacerdotalis,* and the *Responsum Ad Dubium.* Some have claimed that teachings which are set forth or confirmed by the Magisterium without recourse to a definition (a solemn judgment) may be revisable or reformable at a later time, perhaps under another Pontificate. Such an idea is completely lacking in foundation and manifests an erroneous understanding of the doctrine of the Catholic Church regarding the Magisterium.

Indeed, if we consider the *act* of teaching, the Magisterium can teach a doctrine as definitive by an act which is either *defining* or *non-defining.* The Magisterium can proclaim a doctrine as *definitive,* and thus to be believed with divine faith or held definitively, by means of a solemn pronouncement by the Pope *ex cathedra* or by an Ecumenical Council. However, the ordinary papal Magisterium can also teach a doctrine to be *definitive,* as constantly preserved and held by the Tradition and handed on by the ordinary and universal Magisterium. The exercise of the charism of infallibility in this case does not take the form of a defining act by the Roman Pontiff, but instead involves the ordinary and universal Magisterium, which the Pope sums up and sets forth by his formal pronouncement of confirmation and reaffirmation (generally in an encyclical or an apostolic letter). To hold that the Pope must have recourse to an *ex cathedra* definition each and every time he intends to declare a doctrine to be definitive as belonging to the deposit of faith would devalue the ordinary and universal Magisterium and limit infallibility to solemn definitions by a Pope or an Ecumenical Council. This would be an obvious distortion of the teaching of the First and Second Vatican Councils, which both attribute an infallible character to the teachings of the ordinary and universal Magisterium.

With regard to an act of teaching by the papal Magisterium aimed at confirming or reaffirming a certainty of faith that is already consciously lived by the Church or has been set forth by the universal teaching of the entire body of Bishops, the specific *nature* of this act can be seen not *per se* in the doctrine itself, but rather in the fact that the Pope declares that it is a doctrine already belonging to the faith of the Church and infallibly taught by the ordinary and universal Magisterium as divinely revealed or as to be held definitively.

In light of these considerations, it seems that it could be an artificial problem to ask whether the papal act of confirming the ordinary and universal Magisterium is infallible or not. While not being *per se* a *dogmatic definition* (like the Trinitarian dogma of Nicaea, the Christological dogma of Chalcedon, or the Marian dogmas), such a papal pronouncement of confirmation enjoys the same infallibility as the teaching of the ordinary and universal Magisterium, which includes the Pope not simply as one Bishop among many, but as Head of the Episcopal College. In this connection, it is important to clarify that the Congregation's *Responsum Ad Dubium* on the teaching of *Ordinatio Sacerdotalis*, by mentioning the infallible character of a doctrine already in the Church's possession, intended to recall that this teaching was not set forth infallibly only with the publication of the apostolic letter. Rather, *Ordinatio Sacerdotalis* confirmed something which has been held always, everywhere, and by everyone, as belonging to the deposit of the faith. It is essential, therefore, to preserve the principle that a teaching can be set forth infallibly by the ordinary and universal Magisterium, even by an act which does not take the solemn form of a *definition*.

3.   Some have also raised the question of the recognition of a doctrine taught by the ordinary and universal Magisterium as revealed or as to be held definitively. It has been suggested, for example, that such a recognition would require an explicit manifestation of unanimous consent by the entire Episcopal Body, not only in setting forth the specific teaching, but also in declaring its absolute and definitively binding character. Then it is questioned whether such prerequisites have in fact been verified in the case

of the doctrine on the impossibility of conferring priestly ordination on women or with respect to certain universal norms of the natural moral law.

Such questions and doubts, however, do not seem to take adequate account of certain factors which need to be briefly mentioned.

(a) The ordinary and universal Magisterium consists in the morally unanimous teaching of the bishops in communion with the Pope. It is expressed in what *all* the Bishops (including the Bishop of Rome, the Head of the college) attest to in common. It is not a question of extraordinary manifestations, but of the normal life of the Church, of what, without unusual initiatives, is preached as universal teaching in the daily life of the Church: "This ordinary Magisterium is the normal form of the Church's infallibility."[8] It follows therefore that it is by no means necessary that everything that is part of the faith must explicitly become dogma. Instead, it is normal that the mere communality of the proclamation—which includes not only *words* but also *facts*—discloses the truth. The specific and express significance of a dogmatic definition is extraordinary, occasioned in most cases by very particular and precise factors.

(b) Moreover, with regard to the question of verifying the effective consensus of the Bishops spread throughout the world or, what is more, the consensus of the entire Christian people, we must not forget that this *consensus* should not be conceived in a merely *synchronic* sense, but must be understood in its correct *diachronic* sense. This means that a morally *unanimous* consensus embraces all the ages of the Church and only if one listens to this totality does one remain faithful to the apostles. As Joseph Cardinal Ratzinger has noted, "a majority that formed at some juncture against the faith of the Church of all times would be no majority: the true majority in the Church reaches diachronically across the ages."[9]

Thus, it must be remembered that the consensus of the universal Episcopate in communion with the Successor of Peter on the doctrinal and binding character of a statement or practice of the Church in ages past is not annulled or subject to re-evaluation by dissent which arises at a later period.

(c) Finally, with special reference to the teaching regarding the reservation of priestly ordination to men, it must be recalled that the apostolic letter *Ordinatio Sacerdotalis* confirmed that this doctrine has been preserved in the constant and universal Tradition of the Church and has been taught with firmness by the Magisterium in its recent documents (*Ordinatio Sacerdotalis*, no. 4). Tradition is the hermeneutic "place" where the Church's consciousness of truth operates. This consciousness expresses itself in different forms; one of these is the undisturbed conviction regarding a teaching. In the case of the teaching of *Ordinatio Sacerdotalis*, with unanimity and consistency, the Church has never held that women can validly receive priestly ordination. This unanimity and consistency does not reveal an arbitrary decision of the Church, but rather her obedience and dependence on the will of Christ and the apostles. Thus, in the universal Tradition on this question, in its characteristic stability and unanimity, one finds an objective magisterial teaching that is definitive and binding in an unconditional way.[10] The same criteria must be applied as well to other doctrines concerning universal moral norms: the direct and voluntary killing of an innocent human being is always gravely immoral;[11] direct abortion always constitutes a grave moral disorder;[12] euthanasia is a grave violation of the law of God;[13] adultery[14] and calumny are always wrong. These doctrines, which up to now have not been declared by a *solemn judgment*, belong nevertheless to the Church's faith and have been set forth infallibly by the ordinary and universal Magisterium.

In conclusion, to be able to speak of an *infallible, ordinary,* and *universal Magisterium,* the consensus among the Bishops must have as its object a teaching set forth as formally revealed or as certainly true and unquestionable, thus requiring on the part of the Christian faithful full and irrevocable assent. It is the task of theology to conduct serious scholarly research aimed at demonstrating and explaining the existence of such a consensus or agreement. However, there is no foundation for the interpretation which holds that the verification of an infallible teaching of the ordinary and universal Magisterium also requires a particular formality in the declaration of the doctrine in question, for then it would fall in the category of a solemn definition of the Pope or Ecumenical Council.[15]

Today such clarifications appear necessary not in order to respond to subtle and sophisticated academic questions, but in order to refute reductive and simplistic interpretations of the Magisterium's infallibility by providing correct theological principles for interpreting the doctrinal weight of teachings of the Magisterium and the different categories of doctrines.


## III. SOME CONSIDERATIONS ON THE PROBLEM OF PUBLIC DISSENT

Together with these considerations from the doctrinal and theological perspective, it is also opportune to provide some brief reflections and suggestions for remedying the problem of public dissent. It is not possible here to examine the entire range of implications in the pastoral and practical order implied in this question, but it is useful to highlight some fundamental elements which seem to be at the base of this phenomenon. Only thus will we avoid proposing remedies of a merely empirical and episodic character.

1. The basic data cannot be ignored: at the root of dissent is the *crisis of faith*. Therefore, we need to work to reinvigorate the life

of faith. This needs to be a priority of the Church's pastoral activity and it presupposes the call to a greater and ever more profound interior conversion.

2. As one of its first manifestations, the spiritual crisis of faith brings with it *a crisis of obedience to the Magisterium's authority*, which is a crisis in the authority of the Church founded on the divine will. Authority and freedom are artificially set against each other, detaching both from the question of truth.

3. Therefore, the primary remedy is to be found in a serious spiritual, doctrinal, and intellectual formation in conformity with the teaching of the Church.

In this area, some important considerations can be given:

(a) Above all, the urgent need for an *organic and systematic theological formation*. The ever-increasing specialization of theology contributes to its fragmentation, to the point of making theology a *collection of theologies*. Theology in its organic unity risks being lost, and while information in particular areas increases, the essential unifying vision is missing. Similarly, we must insist on the responsibility of Bishops for *catechesis and the formation of catechists*, which must reinforce the sense of the faith and of belonging to the Church.

(b) The necessity of a *solid philosophical formation*, in which the study of metaphysics, which today is lacking in various institutions, is indispensable.[16]

(c) The necessity of re-establishing the proper balance between *the need to protect the rights of the individual* and the need to preserve and *defend the right of the community and of the People of God to the true faith and the common good*. In fact, the real tension is not between defending the rights of the individual and defending the rights of the community. It is rather between those who would protect the rights of the powerful in our culture and those who would defend the rights of the powerless, who are defenseless in the face of the aggressive propagation of opinions in contradiction to the teaching of the Church.

(d) The urgent need to *create a public opinion in the Church* consistent with Catholic identity, free from subjugation to secular public opinion as reflected in the mass media. The Church's openness to the problems of the world needs to be correctly understood: it is based on the missionary impetus that seeks to make known to all the revelation of Jesus Christ and to bring all to the mystery of Christ.

4. From the standpoint of Church discipline, it seems more appropriate than ever to recall that Bishops are required to apply the disciplinary legislation of the Church in an effective way, especially when it is a question of defending the integrity of the teaching of divine truth. This should be done in the context of a new and vigorous re-presentation of the Christian message and of the call to a deeper spiritual life in the service of the new evangelization.

At the present moment in the Church's history, in which the proper consideration of the requirements of law, in particular the norms of canon law, is viewed as somewhat repressive, it is by no means superfluous to emphasize that observance and application of the Church's discipline is not opposed to authentic freedom, nor is it contrary to obedience to the Spirit. It is instead an indispensable instrument for ensuring that communion in truth and love will be effective and ordered. The application of the norms of canon law represents the concrete protection of believers against the falsification of revealed doctrine and the watering-down of the faith caused by that "spirit of the world" which seeks to present itself as the voice of the Holy Spirit.

## IV. The Importance of the *Professio Fidei* and the *Juramentum Fidelitatis*

As is noted in the *Doctrinal Commentary on the Concluding Formula of the* Professio Fidei (1-3),

> From her very beginning, the Church has professed faith in the Lord, crucified and risen, and has gathered the fundamental contents of her belief into certain formulas. The central event of the death and resurrection of the Lord Jesus, expressed first in simple formulas and subsequently in formulas that were more developed, made it possible to give life to that uninterrupted proclamation of faith, in which the Church has handed on both what had been received from the lips of Christ and from his works, as well as what had been learned "at the prompting of the Holy Spirit."

> The same New Testament is the singular witness of the first profession proclaimed by the disciples immediately after the events of Easter: "For I handed on to you as of first importance what I also received: that Christ died for our sins in accordance with the Scriptures; that he was buried; that he was raised on the third day in accordance with the Scriptures; that he appeared to Cephas, then to the Twelve" (1 Cor 15:3-5).

> In the course of the centuries, from this unchangeable nucleus testifying to Jesus as Son of God and as Lord, symbols witnessing to the unity of the faith and to the communion of the churches came to be developed. In these, the fundamental truths which every believer is required to know and to profess were gathered together. Thus, before receiving Baptism, the catechumen must make his profession of faith. The Fathers too, coming together in Councils to respond to historical challenges that required a more complete presentation of the truths of the faith or a defense of the orthodoxy of those truths, formulated new creeds which occupy "a special place in the Church's life" up to the present day. The

diversity of these symbols expresses the richness of the one faith; none of them is superseded or nullified by subsequent professions of faith formulated in response to later historical circumstances.

Christ's promise to bestow the Holy Spirit, who "will guide you into all truth" (Jn 16:13), constantly sustains the Church on her way. Thus, in the course of her history, certain truths have been defined as having been acquired though the Holy Spirit's assistance and are therefore perceptible stages in the realization of the original promise. Other truths, however, have to be understood still more deeply before full possession can be attained of what God, in his mystery of love, wished to reveal to men for their salvation.

In recent times too, in her pastoral care for souls, the Church has thought it opportune to express in a more explicit way the faith of all time. In addition, the obligation has been established for some members of the Christian faithful, called to assume particular offices in the community in the name of the Church, to publicly make a profession of faith according to the formula approved by the Apostolic See.[17]

It is also important to recall that, in 1989, when the new formula of the *Professio Fidei* came into effect, the Congregation also published the *Juramentum Fidelitatis*, which expresses the public commitment to exercise faithfully an office in the Church for those institutions and persons for whom it has been received.[18]

The *Oath of Fidelity,* as in general all observance of canonical legislation, expresses the organic unity between action and governance on one hand, and fidelity to the profession of faith and to Christian truth on the other. In this way, the sense of identity and of belonging to the Church are guaranteed by the law, and the individual believer is prevented from thinking that he belongs to a Church of his own fantasy, constructed according to his own personal standards. We are reminded that we belong to the Church of apostolic succession, the

Church of the Word of God, written and handed down authoritatively, the Church of the visible sacraments and of Catholic communion.

## CONCLUSION

The words of the discourse given by Pope John Paul II to the members of the Congregation for the Doctrine of the Faith at the close of the Plenary Assembly of 1995 are especially enlightening. With regard to the relationship between the Magisterium and theologians, the Pope declared,

> The unity of the faith, for the sake of which the Magisterium has authority and ultimate deliberative power in interpreting the word of God written and handed down, is a primary value, which, if respected, does not involve the stifling of theological research, but provides it with its stable foundation. Theology, in its task of making explicit the intelligible content of the faith, expresses the intrinsic orientation of human intelligence to the truth and the believer's irrepressible need rationally to explore the revealed mystery. To achieve this end, theology can never be reduced to the "private" reflection of a theologian or group of theologians. *The Church is the theologian's vital environment,* and in order to remain faithful to its identity, theology cannot fail to participate deeply in the fabric of the Church's life, doctrine, holiness and prayer. This is the context in which the conviction that theology *needs the living and clarifying word of the Magisterium* becomes fully understandable and perfectly consistent with the logic of Christian faith. The meaning of the Church's Magisterium must be considered *in relation to the truth of Christian doctrine.*[19]

Turning to the relationship between authority and truth—that is, between the exercise of authority and the proclamation of the truth that brings salvation—the Holy Father stated, "The Magisterium, whose authority is exercised in the name of Jesus Christ, is not something independent from or extrinsic to the truth; it is rather an instrument at the service of the truth, a concrete expression of participation in the handing on of the Christian truth in history."[20]

On an existential level, every theologian and every Catholic believer must sense that we Christians live as if carried by the stream of a two thousand-year Tradition. This awareness is the necessary condition for a faith which is truly ecclesial and not merely a private inheritance. Our personal faith has deep roots. With regard to the content of that faith, we are never alone; we are always part of the Church, which keeps a "deposit" and passes it on. Only in such a vision will it seem natural to accept the Church's entire teaching and not just the parts that seem convincing to us. Everything is included when we say "I believe." In different ways, the Church, living in time, makes the content of all times explicit, while at the same time the understanding of the truth develops and makes progress within her. This understanding will be complete only in the eschatological accomplishment of her journey, a journey which at present intersects with the path of the world and its history.

The risk is that passion for the objective search for the truth will languish, and we will close ourselves into our own private solitudes. There is but a single and radical exit from this isolation: the recognition of a truth that transcends us, a truth revealed and given in the Church. Such a recognition is important not only for the community of the Church, but also for the world: truth has a unifying power, which frees us from the enslavement of isolation and creates communion. Obedience to truth is not a suppression of the intellect: it is rather a progressive harmonization of one's mind and heart with the mind and heart of God. We are not saved through self-redemption; we receive the mediation of revelation and grace offered to us by the Church. In the absence of the obedience of faith and the humility to transcend ourselves which it presupposes, there is nothing but the clash of ideologies and the pain of isolation.

# NOTES

1   Cf. Henri de Lubac, "Ecclesia Mater," in *Meditazioni sulla Chiesa* (Milano: Edizioni Paolini, 1955), 275-325; Tarcisio Bertone, "Norma canonica e Magistero ecclesiastico" in *Jus in vita et in missione Ecclesiae* (Vatican City: Libreria Editrice Vaticana, 1994), 1121-1144; M. Masconi, *Magistero autentico non infallibile e protezione penale* (Milano: Edizioni Glossa, 1996); Francis Sullivan, *Magisterium: Teaching Authority in the Catholic Church* (Dublin: Gill and Macmillan, 1983); F. Ardusso, *Magistero ecclesiale* (Milano: Edizioni Paolini, 1997).

2   Cf. Second Vatican Council, dogmatic constitution *Lumen Gentium* (LG), no. 25.

3   "The Roman Pontiff fulfils his universal mission with the help of the various bodies of the Roman Curia and in particular with that of the Congregation for the Doctrine of the Faith in matters of faith and morals. Consequently, the documents issued by this Congregation expressly approved by the Pope participate in the ordinary Magisterium of the Successor of Peter," Congregation for the Doctrine of the Faith, instruction *On the Ecclesial Vocation of the Theologian* (*Donum Veritatis*) (May 24, 1990), 18: *AAS* 82 (1990), 1558.

4   John Paul II, apostolic constitution *Fidei Depositum* (October 11, 1992), 4: *AAS* 86 (1994), 117.

5   Some examples would be the documents published by the Italian Episcopal Conference from 1954 to the present, as collected in the *Enchiridion della Conferenza Episcopale Italiana*, vols. 1-5 (Bologna: EDB, 1985-1996), as well as certain problematic documents such as that of the French Episcopal Conference on the question of AIDS, *Déclaration: SIDA la société en question* (1996); the document of the Committee on Marriage and Family of the National Conference of Catholic Bishops of the United States of America, *Always Our Children* (1997); and finally that of the Commission on Ecumenism of the German Episcopal Conference on the question of Eucharistic Inter-Communion (1997). The pastoral letters of individual Italian Bishops have been collected and published as *Lettere pastorali 1994-1995* (Verona: Edizioni Magistero Episcopale, 1997).

6   Cf. John Paul II, apostolic letter issued *motu proprio Apostolos Suos* (May 21, 1998), 21-22: *AAS* 90 (1998), 654-656.

7   Cf. LG, no. 25.

8   "Dies ordentliche Lehramt ist damit die normale Form der kirchlichen Unfehlbarkeit. . . ," Joseph Cardinal Ratzinger, *Das neue Volk Gottes: Entwürfe zur Ekklesiologie* (Düsseldorf: Patmos-Verlag, 1969), 165.

9   Cardinal Ratzinger, *Called to Communion* (San Francisco: Ignatius Press, 1996), 99.

10  In the past, in fact up to the present decades, theologians and canonists who addressed this question were unanimous in considering the exclusion of women from reception of priestly ordination as something absolute and founded on divine apostolic Tradition. Gasparri can be cited as an example: "Et quidem prohibentur sub poena nullitatis: ita enim traditio et communis doctorum catholicorum doctrina interpretata est legem Apostoli: et ideo Patres inter haereses recensent doctrinam qua sacerdotalis dignitas et officium mulieribus tribuitur," *Tractatus canonicus de sacra ordinatione*, t. 1 (Paris: 1893), 75.

11  Cf. John Paul II, encyclical letter *Evangelium Vitae* (March 25, 1995), 57: *AAS* 87 (1995), 465.

12  Cf. ibid., 62.

13  Cf. ibid., 65.

14  Cf. Second Vatican Council, dogmatic constitution *Gaudium et Spes*, no. 49; *Catechism of the Catholic Church*, no. 2400.

15  Cf. Rm 1:29-30; 1 Cor 6:10; *Catechism of the Catholic Church*, nos. 2477-2479.

16  J. Kleutgen, in his commentary on the second schema on the Church proposed in the First Vatican Council, defines the doctrines of the ordinary infallible Magisterium as those which "are held or handed on as undoubted *(tamquam indubitata tenentur vel traduntur)*" (Mansi, LIII), 313.

17  John Paul II, encyclical letter *Fides et Ratio* (September 14, 1998), 57-63: *AAS* 91 (1999), 50-54.

18  Congregation for the Doctrine of the Faith, *Doctrinal Commentary on the Concluding Formula of the "Professio Fidei"* (June 29, 1998), 1-3: *AAS* 90 (1998), 544-545.

19  Cf. Congregation for the Doctrine of the Faith, *Oath of Fidelity on Assuming an Office to be Exercised in the Name of the Church*: *AAS* 81 (1989), 106.

20  John Paul II, "Discourse to the Participants in the Plenary Assembly of the Congregation for the Doctrine of the Faith," in *L'Osservatore Romano*, English-language edition (November 29, 1995), 3.

21  Ibid., 3.

# COLLABORATION BETWEEN THE CONGREGATION FOR THE DOCTRINE OF THE FAITH AND DOCTRINAL COMMISSIONS OF EPISCOPAL CONFERENCES

## REVEREND ADRIANO GARUTI, OFM

The scope of my intervention will be predominantly technical, namely, to identify in a schematic fashion the criteria for collaboration between the Congregation for the Doctrine of the Faith and the Doctrinal Commissions of Episcopal Conferences in the light of the circular letter of 1990 issued by the Congregation and the apostolic letter *Apostolos Suos,* issued *motu propio* by Pope John Paul II on May 21, 1998.

At the beginning of our analysis, one basic principle needs to be unequivocally clear: Doctrinal Commissions, in their being and their activities, are dependent upon Episcopal Conferences; they are consultative bodies which are responsible to the Conference of Bishops and which assist the Conference in its deliberations of a doctrinal nature. Doctrinal Commissions must always be seen within the framework of the larger context of the Bishops' Conference. The common responsibilities of the Congregation for the Doctrine of the Faith and Doctrinal Commissions derive from their respective functions. The Congregation for the Doctrine of the Faith is that body of the Apostolic See with "the function of promoting and safeguarding doctrine on faith and morals throughout the Catholic world."[1] "In accomplishing this purpose, it renders a service to the truth, by protecting the right of the People of God to receive the Gospel message in its purity and entirety."[2]

As emphasized in the recently published *Regulations for Doctrinal Examination* (1997), "this fundamental pastoral responsibility concerns *all the pastors* of the Church, who have the duty and the right to exercise vigilance, whether individually or gathered in particular Councils or Episcopal Conferences, in order that the faith and morals of the members of the faithful entrusted to their care not suffer harm."[3] To this end, the Bishops are served by Doctrinal Commissions, institutionalized consultative bodies which assist Episcopal Conferences and individual Bishops in their solicitude for the doctrine of the faith. It needs to be remembered that, in keeping with the essential principle of ecclesial subsidiarity, the *Regulations for Doctrinal Examination* foresee that this task of safeguarding the faith will be undertaken principally on the local level, by Bishops and Conferences of Bishops, in each case, by making use of the resources of the Doctrinal Commission. "The principle remains, however, that the Holy See can always intervene and, as a rule, does so when the influence of a publication exceeds the boundaries of an individual Episcopal Conference, or when the danger to the faith is particularly grave."[4]

Therefore, while noting the fundamental difference with regard to the exercise of jurisdiction, it must be noted that there are similarities in structure and purpose between Doctrinal Commissions and the Congregation for the Doctrine of the Faith.

Coming to the topic of this presentation, which is to identify the guidelines for collaboration, it is helpful to recall two documents of the

Congregation, which are now rather distant in time and perhaps somewhat dim in our memory. The first is the instruction published by the Congregation on February 23, 1967, after the reorganization of the Roman Curia under Pope Paul VI; the second is the letter to the Presidents of the Episcopal Conferences issued in the following year, on July 10, 1968. The instruction was intended principally to encourage the setting up of Doctrinal Commissions within each Conference, while the letter sought to specify and facilitate their duties.

The 1967 instruction emphasizes the unity which is to characterize collaboration between the Holy See and the Bishops of the world on doctrinal matters; care for the doctrine of the Catholic faith is something which concerns the entire Church; it is important that Bishops collaborate precisely because they—together with the Roman Pontiff—exercise the apostolic office. What was true in 1967 is even more true today. In our own time, in which advances in knowledge are constantly occurring and in which it is easier than ever before to spread ideas rapidly throughout the world, it is critical that in matters of doctrine Bishops be united among themselves and with the Holy See. The establishment and proper functioning of Doctrinal Commissions can assist immeasurably in responding to this need.

Drawing upon the elements in these two foundational documents and in the light of two decades of experience (in the course of which the new *Code of Canon Law* was promulgated and meetings with Doctrinal Commissions were held in Bogotá, Kinshasa, and Vienna), on November 23, 1990 the Congregation addressed a second circular letter on Doctrinal Commissions to all the Presidents of the Bishops' Conferences of the world. This letter stressed the responsibility of the Conferences to establish Doctrinal Commissions where they did not already exist and sought also to promote their proper functioning. Allow me to call attention to some important elements in this letter.

# I. The Purpose and Organization of Doctrinal Commissions

1. First of all, it must be noted that such Commissions are responsible to and act by mandate of the Episcopal Conferences which have established them. They are consultative bodies instituted to assist the Episcopal Conferences and to assist individual Bishops in their care for the teaching and safeguarding of the faith. The letter makes clear that it is the Bishops who have the primary task as teachers of the Catholic faith. It needs to be emphasized therefore that Doctrinal Commissions, while established by the various conferences of Bishops themselves and at the service of the Conference as such, must also make themselves readily available to individual Bishops.

2. Establishment of a Doctrinal Commission is not absolutely obligatory. In those cases where an Episcopal Conference has a small number of Bishops, it is recommended that the matters which would be dealt with by a Doctrinal Commission be assigned to another Commission. In a subordinate way, the duties of a Doctrinal Commission could be entrusted to a single Bishop who is especially competent in the field.

3. It is obligatory, however, that only Bishops be members of Doctrinal Commissions; theologians or experts can nevertheless be called in from time to time for consultation.

4. The Doctrinal Commission can only make public statements in the name of the entire Conference if it has the explicit authorization to do so. The consultative nature of the Doctrinal Commission should not be overlooked.

5. It is recommended, though not mentioned in the circular letter, that the duration of the terms of the Bishop members of the Doctrinal Commission be arranged in order to avoid a situation

in which all the members come to the end of their terms at the same time. Terms of office should end in successive stages to guarantee continuity in programs and activities.

## II. THE VARIOUS FUNCTIONS OF DOCTRINAL COMMISSIONS

The circular letter of 1990 goes on to list the tasks of a Doctrinal Commission. These are similar, in many cases, to those of the Congregation for the Doctrine of the Faith. They are not abstract; they are determined by the needs of the moment in history in which we live.

1.  In addressing the concrete needs of our day and age, the Doctrinal Commissions can make use of the documents issued by the Holy See, especially those published by the Congregation for the Doctrine of the Faith. These documents can be distributed, reprinted, commented upon, and even adapted by the Doctrinal Commissions. The number of documents issued by the Congregation in the past few years has been quite significant. It is necessary that these efforts of the Congregation be matched by those of the various Conferences of Bishops. There can always be greater collaboration in this area.

I should note that more than ten years ago, the Congregation published a volume containing the documents produced from 1966 to 1985, that is, in the first twenty years after the Council.[5] The Congregation is currently working on a second volume which will include those published between 1986 and 2000, approximately thirty documents. In addition to these books, the Congregation has been publishing a series of smaller volumes, entitled *Documenti e Studi*, which present specific documents of the Holy See together with relevant articles of explanation and illustration. Ten of these volumes have now been published. The Congregation would like to see these translated into the major languages. In Spain, the publishers of the magazine *Palabra* have been translating the volumes as they appear. In October 1996, the Congregation wrote to the Bishops' Conferences of France, Germany, and the United States of America, asking if they might arrange for the translation and publication of the volume entitled *Dall'Inter Insigniores all'Ordinatio Sacerdotalis*. The Conference of Bishops of the United States subsequently produced an excellent translation in March 1998. In June of that same year, the Congregation was approached by Mr. Fergus Martin, General Secretary of the Catholic Truth Society (CTS) in England, who explained that his publishing house would be interested in translating the entire series. He later made the necessary contact with the Libreria Editrice Vaticana, which holds the copyright on the volumes. Unfortunately, however, the Catholic Truth Society has very limited distribution outside Great Britain and the Commonwealth. For this reason, Mr. Martin explained that he would be in contact with the Bishops' Conference of the United States and possibly also with a publisher such as Ignatius Press in order to propose co-publication of the series or distribution in the United States of the volumes published by the CTS.

2.  A specific task of Doctrinal Commissions is that of exercising vigilance over writings and, more generally, over the use made of the various means of communication with regard to matters of faith and morals. In this area, the Congregation published in 1992 an instruction entitled *Some Aspects of the Use of the Instruments of Social Communication in Promoting the Doctrine of the Faith,* which refers to the "invaluable aid which they [Doctrinal Commissions] can offer to Bishops in the fulfilment of their teaching mission."[6] One area of assistance can be with regard to Catholic publishing. Because of the possibilities for wide distribution of books and printed materials, Catholic publishing houses are an enormous resource, one of the greatest in fact, which the Church possesses for the promotion of her teaching. At the present moment, however, Catholic publishing houses at times present problems because in certain cases they operate with little sense of doctrinal accountability. A situation should not be

permitted to arise in which a member of the Catholic faithful buys a book printed by a Catholic publishing house which turns out to be clearly inconsistent with authentic Catholic doctrine. In fact, "Catholic publishers are not to issue works which do not have the prescribed ecclesiastical permission."[7] Because the sheer volume of the publications of a Catholic publisher may tax, if not completely overwhelm, the theological resources of a small Diocese, the Doctrinal Commission of the Conference should assist in the work of evaluation for ecclesiastical permission.

As we know, the circular letter of 1990 states that Doctrinal Commissions should assist Bishops in their task of evaluating books which have been submitted for the *imprimatur*; at the very least, the Doctrinal Commissions should draw up lists of theological experts which could be provided to individual Bishops. If these steps are taken, it would significantly reduce the number of cases in which the Congregation has to intervene regarding errors contained in books that have received an *imprimatur.*

3.  I would now like to turn to what is one of the most important of the services which Doctrinal Commissions are asked to render to the Bishops. The letter of 1990 states, "The Doctrinal Commissions are also called to promote the work of theology. To this end, then, they should foster good mutual relations with theologians, teachers in universities and seminaries, indeed with all experts in the ecclesiastical disciplines." Here we are dealing with the important topic of the relationship between the Magisterium and theologians.

The Congregation, for its part, sought to promote such collaboration with its instruction *On the Ecclesial Vocation of the Theologian* (*Donum Veritatis*), a document which speaks of the reciprocal relationship between the Magisterium and theologians.[8] Here too, the Doctrinal Commission, by fulfilling its proper functions, can promote this relationship in various ways and assist the Bishops in their dealings with theologians. The Doctrinal Commission should watch over the activities of associations of theologians and keep the other Bishops informed of developments. The Doctrinal Commission can also be of assistance to local Bishops when, as required by canon law, a theologian requests the *mandatum* from the competent ecclesiastical authority in order to teach theology in a Catholic college or university.[9]

4.   This point leads me to recall the duties of Doctrinal Commissions in relation to other commissions of the Episcopal Conference, especially those concerned with education (in seminaries, universities, and schools), as well as Commissions on Liturgy and Ecumenism. These are all areas of significant doctrinal importance. The Doctrinal Commission of the Bishops' Conference should be involved in ensuring that seminaries, universities, and schools be places where correct doctrinal teaching is received. It should also work in collaboration with the Liturgical Commission, especially on the question of the doctrinal fidelity of proposed liturgical translations. With respect to seminaries, the Doctrinal Commission could be involved in establishing a list of approved textbooks. In the area of ecumenism, the Doctrinal Commission should play a central role in the evaluation of ecumenical agreements which may be under consideration by the Conference or by individual Bishops. It should also be noted—as the circular letter states—that normally the other Commissions of the Conference should not publish important documents without first having received the judgment of the Doctrinal Commission in what pertains to its competence.

5.   The Doctrinal Commissions of different countries, especially those of the same geographical area or sharing a common language, should find ways of exchanging information and promoting collaboration. This, of course, is one of the principal aims of our meeting here in Menlo Park.

6. Furthermore, as the circular letter notes, it would be very helpful if the President of each Doctrinal Commission would prepare an annual report for the Congregation for the Doctrine of the Faith on the work of the Commission and on the doctrinal questions of greatest importance in that particular country; suggestions could be included regarding the best way for the Holy See to address such questions. The practice of the annual report is an effective way to further the relationship of collaboration which is evident in our meeting.

Close collaboration is so important that I would even suggest the appropriateness of periodic meetings in Rome between the Congregation for the Doctrine of the Faith and Doctrinal Commissions. This is already happening with several Doctrinal Commissions from Europe and with the Presidents of the Bishops' Conferences of the United States and Canada. These regular meetings have proved invaluable in the solution of a number of difficult doctrinal questions.

7. Finally, in light of the apostolic letter *Apostolos Suos*, I would like to offer some brief reflections on the question of the doctrinal competence of Episcopal Conferences and of their reciprocal relationship with their Doctrinal Commissions.

The apostolic letter, after having cited the relevant canons of the *Code of Canon Law* which delineate areas of doctrinal competence, explains the nature and limits of this competence: "The Bishops, assembled in Episcopal Conference, must take special care to follow the Magisterium of the universal Church and to communicate it opportunely to the people entrusted to them."[10] This statement is followed by a clarification which perhaps constitutes the true novelty of the document: "when the doctrinal declarations of Episcopal Conferences are approved unanimously, they may certainly be issued in the name of the Conferences themselves, and the faithful are obliged to adhere with a sense of religious respect to that authentic magisterium."[11] In the absence, however, of such a unanimity, it is necessary that they receive the *recognitio* of the Holy See. These paragraphs therefore contain an explicit recognition of the doctrinal competence of Bishops' Conferences, while specifying that the teaching of the Conferences, though certainly authentic, will seek to make known to the faithful the teaching set forth by the universal Magisterium.

More specific pronouncements by Bishops' Conferences that are aimed at resolving new questions arising from changes in society would not assume a similar universal character. Such statements can serve to pave the way for the universal Magisterium, when on a determined point, moral certainty has not yet been reached and therefore a pronouncement by the Church on a higher magisterial level is not advisable. To give one example among many, I would mention the question of the medical treatment of anencephalic infants. On this issue, the Congregation approached Bishop Anthony M. Pilla, who was then President of the Episcopal Conference of the United States, with the request that the Committee on Doctrine of the Conference develop and publish a document which would address the moral aspects of this question. In 1996, the Doctrinal Committee published *Moral Principles Concerning Infants with Anencephaly;*[12] the text was later printed in *L'Osservatore Romano* (1998). The staff of the Committee on Doctrine also published a commentary on this document entitled *Anencephalic Infants and Their Care.*[13] While being official and authentic statements in communion with the Apostolic See and of great practical value for the Church, they do not have the characteristics of an act of the universal Magisterium.

In summary, the Conferences of Bishops, in the exercise of their magisterial office, can be assisted by other bodies, such as their Doctrinal Commissions. These bodies, however, "do not have the authority to carry out acts of authentic magisterium either in their own name or in the name of the Conference, and not even as a task assigned to them by the Conference."[14] Having noted this, however, the Doctrinal

Commission can be authorized by the Permanent Council of the Conference to release statements which would not be acts of authentic magisterium.[15]

Following these criteria, we should not find it difficult to promote a relationship of effective collaboration between the Congregation for the Doctrine of the Faith and the various Doctrinal Commissions, a relationship which, in a common spirit of service, will promote and safeguard Catholic doctrine on faith and morals throughout the world. Allow me to conclude by proposing that we might discuss this question of collaboration between the Congregation and Doctrinal Commissions and thus arrive at some specific recommendations for incorporation into the conclusions of our meeting.

# NOTES

1   John Paul II, apostolic constitution *Pastor Bonus* (June 28, 1998), 48: *AAS* 80 (1988), 873.

2   Congregation for the Doctrine of the Faith, *Agendi ratio in doctrinarum examine* (June 29, 1997), art. 1: *AAS* 89 (1997), 830.

3   Ibid., art. 2.

4   Ibid., art. 2.

5   *Documenta inde a Concilio Vaticano Secundo expleto edita (1966-1985)* (Vatican City: Libreria Editrice Vaticana, 1985).

6   Congregation for the Doctrine of the Faith, instruction on *Some Aspects of the Use of the Instruments of Social Communication in Promoting the Doctrine of the Faith* (March 30, 1992), in *Enchiridion Vaticanum* 13: 869.

7   Ibid., 874.

8   Congregation for the Doctrine of the Faith, instruction *On the Ecclesial Vocation of the Theologian* (*Donum Veritatis*) (May 24, 1990), 40: *AAS* 82 (1990), 1569.

9   Cf. *Code of Canon Law,* can. 812.

10  John Paul II, apostolic letter issued *motu proprio Apostolos Suos* (AS) (May 21, 1998), 21: *AAS* 90 (1998), 655.

11  Ibid., 22.

12  *Origins* 26 (October 10, 1996), 276.

13  *L'Osservatore Romano*, English-language edition (September 23, 1998), 7.

14  AS, 23; cf. Complementary Norm 2: *AAS* 90 (1998), 656.

15  Ibid., *Norms*, art. 2-3: 657.

# SOME BRIEF RESPONSES TO QUESTIONS REGARDING THE *PROFESSIO FIDEI*

1. Because the truths of the second paragraph of the *Professio Fidei* are described as "definitive," does it follow that these truths can also be described as "irreformable"?

**Affirmative.**

The word "definitive" was chosen because this is the term used in *Lumen Gentium*, no. 25, which speaks of *sententia definitive tenenda*. The word "irreformable," on the other hand, was used in the dogmatic constitution *Pastor Aeternus* of the First Vatican Council with regard to dogmatic definitions. There is no essential difference between the two terms with regard to their conceptual substance. At the same time, however, in both cases—that is, regarding irreformable dogmatic definitions and doctrines which are to be held definitively—the Church teaches that, while the meaning and conceptual content must always remain the same, these truths may come to be expressed in language that is more complete and more perfect (cf. Congregation for the Doctrine of the Faith, *Mysterium Ecclesiae*, no. 5).

2. Is it true that every doctrine which has been set forth definitively must also be considered as having been taught infallibly?

**Affirmative.**

It would be contradictory for the Magisterium to require, by an act that is not infallible, firm and definitive assent to a doctrine set forth as divinely revealed or as intrinsically necessary for keeping and expounding the deposit of faith. It must be remembered, however, that it is a doctrine of the Church's faith that the Magisterium can teach a doctrine infallibly both by an act that is defining (i.e., in solemn form) or by an act that is not defining (i.e., in ordinary form).

- The first case is that of an *ex cathedra* definition by the Roman Pontiff or a solemn pronouncement by an Ecumenical Council.

- The second case is that of a teaching of the ordinary and universal Magisterium, which can be formally reaffirmed or confirmed by the ordinary Magisterium of the Pope (see, e.g., Pope Paul VI's *Credo of the People of God* [1968], the apostolic letter *Ordinatio Sacerdotalis,* or the three pronouncements found in the encyclical letter *Evangelium Vitae*).

The essential point is that *the Magisterium can teach a doctrine infallibly without necessarily having recourse to the form of a (solemn) definition.*

3. Does the second paragraph of *Professio Fidei* correspond to what was previously called "the secondary object of infallibility"?

To respond to this question, some distinctions have to be made. If by the "secondary object of infallibility" is meant exclusively the area of truths of a rational or natural order—as perhaps was maintained by certain currents of the post-Tridentine theology of the manuals—then it is clear that the truths of the second paragraph of the *Professio Fidei* go beyond this area and would include other doctrines as well. However, if by the "secondary object of infallibility" is meant the area of doctrines that have a necessary logical or historical connection with divine Revelation, then the answer to the question must be affirmative. Furthermore, the process of dogmatic development illustrates how, in the consciousness of the Church, the understanding of the realities and the words of the deposit of faith can progress to the point where the Magisterium may proclaim some of these doctrines as dogmas of divine and Catholic faith—including elements that previously had not been expressly recognized as revealed.

It would be helpful, therefore, to recall that the area of the truths belonging to the second paragraph includes doctrines of various types. They can be described as follows:

- Doctrines concerning faith and morals that the Church holds as definitive, although they have not been expressly and categorically set forth as divinely revealed. This does not exclude the possibility that in the course of dogmatic development the Magisterium could, at a later point, proclaim such doctrines as dogmas of divine and Catholic faith. Examples of these would include the doctrine of the primacy of jurisdiction of the Roman Pontiff in the period before the dogmatic proclamation of the First Vatican Council; the impossibility of conferring priestly ordination on women; the sacramentality of the Diaconate and the Episcopate taught at the Second Vatican Council, but not set forth as a dogma of faith; and the doctrines that refer to the universal negative moral norms prohibiting intrinsically evil acts.

- Doctrines or facts that the Church proposes infallibly to be held definitely, even though they are not formally revealed. Examples of these would be the canonization of saints; the judgment on the invalidity of the present rite of Anglican ordinations; and the legitimacy of a particular ecumenical council. These are based ultimately on faith in the Holy Spirit's assistance to the Church and on the Catholic doctrine of the infallibility of the Magisterium.

- Doctrines concerning faith and morals, which have been obtained by the addition of true elements—though not formally revealed—to other elements deriving directly from Revelation. Examples would include the condemnation of the positions of Jansen; the teaching of the Council of Constance, which defined as theologically certain the licitness of reception of Holy Communion under only one species; the condemnation of those who believe that the secret confession of sins to a priest is opposed to the teaching of Christ; the anathema of those who would affirm that marital indissolubility, as understood by the Catholic Church, is contrary to the Gospel; and the philosophical possibility of demonstrating the existence of God or the spiritual nature and immortality of the human soul.

The distinction between the two paragraphs, corresponding to the respective orders of truth, does not introduce an addition or an extrinsic quantitative increase of doctrine to the deposit of faith. Rather, it seeks to specify more precisely the different relationships that—within the deposit of the faith—individual doctrines have with the foundation and the center of divine Revelation.

4.  Could the teaching of *Ordinatio Sacerdotalis* belong to the first paragraph of the *Professio Fidei*?

The Doctrinal Commission of the Second Vatican Council explained the text of *Lumen Gentium*, no. 25, regarding the object of infallibility in the following words: "*Obiectum infallibilitatis Ecclesiae . . . eamdem habet extensionem ac depositum revelatum; ideoque extenditur ad ea omnia, et ad ea tantum, quae vel directe ad ipsum depositum revelatum spectant, vel quae ad idem depositum sancte custodiendum et fideliter exponendum requiruntur . . .*" (*Acta Synodalia Sacrosancti Concilii Oecumenici Vaticani II*, vol. III, no. I, 251). This means that the doctrines that relate to the deposit of the faith are not only those that directly belong to it, but also the doctrines necessary for the integral preservation of that deposit.

The difference between the truths of the first paragraph and those of the second is not therefore to be found in the fact that only the first are contained in the deposit of the faith, but rather in the fact that the first, since they are directly revealed, are expressly set forth as such by the infallible Magisterium. The second are set forth infallibly in a definitive way, because they are necessarily connected to divine Revelation either by virtue of a logical or historical relationship. Thus, in the final analysis, the definitive character of such statements (of the second paragraph) derives from Revelation itself.

The doctrine of *Ordinatio Sacerdotalis* can be held legitimately by theologians to be a doctrine of divine and Catholic faith (i.e., as belonging to the first paragraph). For the moment, however, the Magisterium has simply reaffirmed it as a truth of the Church's doctrine (the second paragraph), based on Scripture, attested to and applied in the uninterrupted Tradition, and taught by the ordinary and universal Magisterium, without declaring it to be a dogma that is divinely revealed.

Therefore, it is not contrary to the Magisterium to classify this doctrine as a truth of divine and Catholic faith; such a claim is, however, for the moment a theological opinion. On the other hand, it would be contrary to the teaching of the Church to maintain that this doctrine belongs to the third paragraph and as such requires only religious submission of intellect and will, and not a firm and irrevocable assent. For example, before the proclamation of the dogma of the Assumption of the Mother of God, it was legitimate in theology, though not obligatory, to maintain that this teaching was a doctrine that was divinely revealed; but it was not legitimate to cast doubt on the teaching itself or to maintain that it was only a prudential teaching and thus open to revision.

5.  Is it possible to hold the position that the Magisterium does not have the capacity to teach infallibly regarding particular applications of the natural moral law?

The instruction *Donum Veritatis* (no. 16) of the Congregation for the Doctrine of the Faith states the following:

> By reason of the connection between the orders of creation and redemption, and by reason of the necessity, in view of salvation, of knowing and observing the whole moral law, the competence of the Magisterium also extends to that which concerns the natural law (cf. *Humanae vitae*, 4). Revelation also contains moral teachings which *per se* could be known by natural reason. Access to them, however, is made difficult by man's sinful condition. It is a doctrine of the faith that these moral norms can be infallibly taught by the Magisterium (cf. *Dei filius*, chapter 2; DS 3005).

So given that the observance of all negative moral norms that concern intrinsically evil acts (*intrinsece mala*) is necessary for salvation, it follows that the Magisterium has the competence to teach infallibly and to make obligatory the definitive assent of the members of the faithful with regard to the knowledge and application in life of these norms. This judgment belongs to the Catholic doctrine on the infallibility of the Magisterium.

With regard to the particular application of the norms of the natural moral law that do not have a necessary connection with Revelation— for example, numerous positive moral norms that are valid *ut in pluribus*—it has not been defined nor is it binding that the Magisterium can teach infallibly in such specific matters.

6.   The "Doctrinal Commentary on the *Professio Fidei*" states that a person who denies a truth of the second paragraph would no longer be in full communion with the Church. Does it follow from this that such a person cannot be admitted to the sacraments?

**Negative.**

*Ad Tuendam Fidem* chapter 4 (part A) gives the new version of canon 1371, 1° of the *Code of Canon Law*; it speaks of "a just penalty."

# National Conference of Catholic Bishops (USA)

# THE ROLE OF THE THEOLOGIAN IN A CATHOLIC COLLEGE OR UNIVERSITY IN THE LIGHT OF *AD TUENDAM FIDEM* AND THE *PROFESSIO FIDEI*

### MOST REVEREND DANIEL E. PILARCZYK

There is a close affinity between theologians and the hierarchical magisterium because both are concerned with understanding divine truth in human language. But the close affinity should not be an occasion for confusion—for obliterating the difference. The magisterium, and it alone, has the power and the responsibility to formulate doctrine in a binding way that calls for the assent of the faithful. The magisterium speaks with the authority that derives from the charism of office. The pope has a specific charism that has been called the *veritatis et fidei numquam deficientis charisma* (Vatican I, Denzinger Schönmetzer [DS], no. 3071). Thanks to their ordination and canonical mission, bishops in union with the pope enjoy what Irenaeus and Vatican II call *charisma veritatis certum* (*Dei Verbum* [DV], no. 8).[1] While the fruitful exercise of this charism depends on personal qualifications and application, the Lord sees to it that, notwithstanding the personal deficiencies of individual popes and bishops, the magisterium as a whole does not lead the Church astray.

The authority of the theologian is more difficult to specify, especially because the term "theologian" is so broadly used in current discourse. Is the theologian necessarily a believer? Must he or she be a baptized Christian? Must the theologian have engaged in formal study on an advanced level? If so, can the competence of the theologian be certified by a secular degree from a Catholic institution, by a degree from a secular institution, or by one from a Protestant seminary or an ecumenical consortium? Distinctions must be made in responding to questions such as these.

For purposes of this paper, a Catholic theologian will be defined as an orthodox Catholic believer who has a demonstrated capacity to teach or write in a scholarly way about the themes of Christian revelation from the perspective of Catholic faith. The required competence may be indicated presumptively by a graduate degree in theology conferred by an approved Catholic institution—one able to confer the title of master, the licentiate, or the doctorate. But in particular cases competence may be demonstrated in other ways, for example, by the quality of a person's writing. For professors of theology in Catholic institutions a *mandatum docendi* or *missio canonica* is normally expected (cf. can. 812).

The purpose of theology is to achieve and disseminate a mature critical understanding of the foundations, content, practical applications, and theoretical implications of Christian revelation as handed down in Scripture and Tradition and as certified by the ecclesiastical magisterium. By enhancing the understanding of faith, theology can pave the way for developments of Christian doctrine.

The description of theology here offered is deliberately very broad. It allows for multiple specializations: apologetical, biblical, historical, systematic (speculative), pastoral, moral, mystical, ecumenical, missiological, etc. A given theologian might be a specialist in some area, such as sacraments, or in some period, such as the medieval period.

In the Middle Ages, when the Catholic character of theology could be taken for granted, theology flourished in universities that had official links with the hierarchy (either the local bishop or the Holy See). Theologians of various nationalities, while belonging to different schools, formed a loosely knit community, sometimes known as the *schola theologorum*. The *consensus theologorum* was considered to be a solid indication of orthodoxy. Suspect opinions were often submitted to theological faculties for an opinion before being censured by the hierarchy.

In countries such as the United States today the situation of university theology is very different. The faculty consists not only of clergy and religious but to a large and increasing extent of lay men and women, many of whom do not hold ecclesiastical degrees, and some of whom are not Catholics or even Christians (e.g., professors of Judaic studies). Many Catholic universities do not have a theology department, but only a department of religious studies, in which religion is scientifically studied as a phenomenon, with the tools of philosophy, history, psychology, sociology, and the like. Those that do have "theology" departments do not necessarily insist on courses being taught from the perspective of faith, let alone Catholic faith, although some professors of course do teach from a consciously Catholic point of view. Even the Catholic professors are likely to have their degrees from non-Catholic institutions and to have specialized in the writing of non-Catholic theologians. It cannot be taken for granted, therefore, that even the Catholic members of the theology department have more than a superficial knowledge of the Catholic tradition or that they are personally committed to all the doctrines of the Church.

In many universities the Catholic character of the theology curriculum has been greatly attenuated since Vatican II. Some of the reasons for this are social and economic. To attract good students and even in some cases to survive, Catholic universities are anxious to receive favorable ratings by secular or non-Catholic accrediting associations, which may require that they have a faculty with degrees from prestigious universities and that they be institutionally independent of any ecclesiastical controls. They generally wish to be eligible for federal and state funding, which may require them to be classified as "equal opportunity employers" and to avoid "indoctrinating" students in a "sectarian" way. They may wish to reach out to a broader student body, within which Catholics may perhaps be a minority.

For many reasons such as those just mentioned, it has become much more difficult than it was a generation or two ago to identify Catholic university theology. The kind of collaboration between the magisterium and theological faculties that was customary in the late Middle Ages is not easy to realize in our day. Hallowed concepts such as the *schola theologorum* and the *consensus theologorum* are difficult to apply. Many theologians do of course collaborate with bishops and with the Holy See, but they are selected on an individual basis, not as representatives of the theological community.

Possibly the situation would be changed if there were Catholic accrediting agencies that would evaluate the Catholic character of university education and if something like the *mandatum docendi* mentioned in canon 812 in the code of 1983 were in force. But many university officials maintain that these measures would seriously impede the good that Catholic universities are now accomplishing. To make recommendations about accrediting associations and the *mandatum* lies beyond the scope of this paper, which is concerned with the Profession of Faith, the Congregation for the Doctrine of the Faith (CDF) "Commentary on the Profession of Faith," and the apostolic letter *Ad Tuendam Fidem*.

The question does of course arise whether teachers of theology or religious studies in non-ecclesiastical faculties are obliged to make the Profession of Faith. In practice they rarely do so unless they have been ordained to the diaconate in the past decade. The preponderance of canonical opinion seems to hold that there is no clear obligation for professors to take the oath unless they teach in Catholic institutions under the control of the Church. There is widespread disagreement about which institutions are truly under the control of the Church. In any case, the code does not impose any penalty for failure to make the Profession of Faith even when it is required.

The Profession of Faith of 1989 replaced a much briefer and simpler profession drawn up in 1967, which consisted simply of a recitation of the Nicene-Constantinoplitan Creed followed by the sentence:

> I firmly embrace and accept all and everything that has been either defined by the Church's solemn deliberations or affirmed and declared by its ordinary magisterium concerning the doctrine of faith and morals, according as they are proposed by it, especially those things dealing with the mystery of Holy Church of Christ, its sacraments and the sacrifice of the Mass, and the primacy of the Roman Pontiff.

This profession did not make any distinction between revealed truths and non-revealed truths concerning faith and morals. It restricted itself to solemn teachings of popes and councils and to teachings of the ordinary magisterium. It said nothing of authentic teaching that is not irreformable.

The 1983 code, in canon 750, affirms the need to believe the Word of God both as solemnly defined and as taught by the ordinary and universal magisterium, but it makes no mention of non-revealed truths taught as necessarily connected with revelation. In canon 752 the code teaches the obligation to submit with religious *obsequium* of intellect and will to  nondefinitive teachings of the magisterium. In canon 1364 it provides for the excommunication of those who culpably reject teachings that are of faith. In canon 1371 (1) the code provides penalties for those who pertinaciously reject other authentic Catholic teachings.

The Profession of Faith of 1989 makes a further advance in distinguishing among three levels of authority in Catholic teaching and specifies three levels of assent corresponding to these levels. The three kinds of doctrine are revealed truths that are definitively taught as being revealed; truths that, although not themselves revealed, are intimately or necessarily connected with revelation and are definitively taught as such by the Church; and authentic Catholic teaching that makes no claim to be definitive. The response of the Catholic faithful to these levels of doctrine is gradated. To the first category, the response is the assent of faith, *obsequium fidei*. To the second category, the appropriate response is a firm or definitive assent. To the third category, the response is, in the terminology of Vatican II, *religiosum voluntatis et intellectus obsequium*.

A Catholic theologian, like any other Catholic, may be expected to give the appropriate response to teachings on all three levels. Theologians who manifestly fail to do so must be considered deficient precisely in their quality as Catholic theologians. For the Catholic theologian, as we have seen, reflects on the deposit of faith in the light of Catholic tradition under the guidance of the magisterium. The theologian does not construct Christian doctrine but receives that doctrine from the sacred sources and seeks to understand and interpret it.

The threefold classification of Catholic teaching in the two documents on which I am here commenting should offer no difficulty. The first category includes the articles of the creed, the defined dogmas of popes and ecumenical councils, and those truths constantly taught by the bishops in their ordinary and universal magisterium. All of these loci are recognized as infallible by the First and Second Vatican Councils, and this recognition has gained general acceptance in the Catholic theological world.

The articles of the creed and the dogmas of the Church—even those not solemnly defined—are obligatory on all Catholics, in the sense that to doubt or deny them deliberately is a rupture of Catholic communion, excluding a person from full incorporation in the Church (cf. *Lumen Gentium* [LG], no. 14). Catholic dogmatic or systematic theology must proceed on the assumption that the articles of the creed and the dogmas of the Church are true and revealed, though of course methodic doubt is a legitimate device for obtaining or imparting a better understanding of these truths. Although there are no limits to the questions that can be raised in Catholic theology, the theologian is aware that any answers, to be viable in Catholic theology, must be in harmony with the whole system of Catholic dogma.

In the mid-nineteenth century Ignaz Döllinger and some of his associates in Germany sought to limit the dogmatic teaching of the Church to defined dogmas, but Pius IX reacted promptly in the letter *Tuas Libenter*, which asserted that the ordinary and universal teaching of the bishops is likewise a matter of faith (DS, no. 2879). This doctrine of Pius IX was incorporated in the teaching of Vatican I (*Dei Filius*, DS, no. 3011) and was repeated by Vatican II (LG, no. 25). The clarity achieved thanks to these documents is a true development that cannot without regression be thrown into doubt.

The Fathers at Vatican I and Vatican II agreed that the infallibility of the magisterium was not restricted to revealed truths. At Vatican I the dogmatic constitution *Pastor Aeternus* spoke not simply of *credenda* (revealed truths to be accepted by divine and Catholic faith) but also of *tenenda* (truths to be firmly held because they were intimately connected with revelation and infallibly taught). The latter were understood to be included within the scope of truths that the successors of Peter *sancte custodirent et fideliter exponerent* (*Pastor Aeternus*, DS, no. 3070).

Vatican I did not decide the disputed question whether these other truths, in order to be infallibly taught, had to be *necessarily* connected with revealed truths. The same openness was left at Vatican II, which used the consecrated terms *sancte custodiendum et fideliter exponendum* (LG, no. 25). The Theological Commission held that the magisterium was infallible in teaching truths that pertained not only directly but also indirectly to the deposit of faith. It interpreted the Latin phrase just quoted as meaning that the object of infallibility extends to truths that are not formally contained in the revealed deposit, but are required for the deposit to be religiously safeguarded and faithfully expounded.[2]

The CDF in its declaration *Mysterium Ecclesiae* (1973) was even more specific:

> According to Catholic doctrine, the infallibility of the magisterium of the Church extends not only to the deposit of faith, but also to those matters without which this deposit cannot be properly preserved and expounded. (no. 3)

The Profession of Faith of 1989, in a paragraph following the enumeration of truths to be believed on a motive of faith, seems to have this secondary object of infallibility in mind when it requires that one "firmly accept and hold each and every thing that is proposed by the same [Church] definitively with regard to teaching concerning faith and morals." The CDF *Instruction on the Ecclesial Vocation of the Theologian*, in similar language, speaks of truths "strictly and intimately connected with revelation" (*Donum Veritatis*, 23). The CDF commentary on the last three paragraphs of the Profession of Faith explains that the truths to be "firmly accepted and held" include "all those teachings belonging to the dogmatic or moral area which are necessary for faithfully keeping and expounding the deposit of faith, even if they have not been proposed by the magisterium of the Church as formally revealed."[3]

The Profession of 1989 made an advance by mentioning all three categories of Catholic doctrine and distinguishing among the responses due to each. This advance, in turn, called for a minor adjustment in the *Code of Canon Law* regarding the second category. The question was whether a failure to assent to definitive but non-revealed doctrine was to be treated canonically in the same way as heresy, or as equivalent to the failure to accept authentic but nondefinitive doctrine, or in some intermediate way.

John Paul II, in his apostolic letter *Ad Tuendam Fidem*, no. 3, addressed this problem. In amending the code he adopted the most moderate of the three options. Canon 750, dealing with infallible teaching, is amended by adding a new clause mentioning truths that are not themselves revealed but are "required for the sacred preservation and faithful explanation of the same deposit of faith." The amendment to canon 1371§1 calls for the rejection of teachings in the second category to be treated canonically in the same way as the rejection of teachings in the third category.[4] In describing doctrines of the second category, canon 750 §2, in the amended version, states that these truths must be "intimately linked" with revealed truths "either for historical reasons or through logical connection."[5]

It seems evident that the charism of infallibility, if given for revealed truths, must extend also to truths that are necessarily presupposed by, or necessarily linked with, the deposit of faith, for otherwise the magisterium's power to teach would be rendered ineffectual. As an example of a truth historically connected with revelation one may mention facts such as the validity of papal elections or ecumenical councils. If it could always be questioned whether a given council was ecumenical or whether a given pope was validly elected, the teachings of infallible councils and popes could be contested. As a truth logically connected with revelation one could adduce the idea that human knowledge can extend to things spiritual and divine. If human knowledge could never attain certitude without empirical verification, the entire teaching of the Church about God would be called into question. To deny truths immediately and necessarily connected with revelation is, moreover, to diminish the illuminative power of revelation itself.

The appropriate response to truths necessarily connected with revelation, and taught as such by the Church, cannot be the assent of divine and Catholic faith, for this assent goes out only to the Word of God. Yet it must be a firm, definitive assent, or faith itself would be weakened. Thus it seems clear that the *Code of Canon Law*, the Profession of Faith, and *Ad Tuendam Fidem* have correctly identified the response as one of "firmly holding and accepting" these teachings.

The third category is no more problematic than the preceding two. There is a vast body of Catholic teaching, for example in papal encyclicals, for which no claim of infallibility or definitiveness is made. Such teaching is authoritative, at least when the magisterium explicitly or implicitly claims to be teaching in the name of Christ. The kind of assent due to such teaching was not much discussed until the middle of the present century, when Pius XII in *Humani Generis* dealt with the authority of encyclicals in which the pope does not exercise the supreme power of his magisterium but nevertheless deliberately passes judgment on a matter hitherto controverted. He said that in such cases, "in accordance with the mind and intention of the same Pontiffs, that question can no longer be considered a subject for free debate among theologians" (DS, no. 3885).

Vatican II in *Lumen Gentium*, no. 25, did not repeat this statement about closing off theological debate, but it did say that the ordinary papal magisterium calls for *religiosum voluntatis et intellectus obsequium*. Some authors translate *obsequium* as "assent" or "obedience"; others as "respect" or "reverence." The CDF instruction *On the Ecclesial Vocation of the Theologian* (*Donum Veritatis*) casts some further light on the interpretation of this difficult term by stating: "This kind of response cannot be simply exterior and disciplinary, but must be understood within the logic of faith and under the impulse of obedience to the faith" (no. 23). In no. 24, *Donum Veritatis* goes on to state, still more significantly:

> The willingness to submit loyally to the teaching of the magisterium on matters not *per se* irreformable must be the rule. It can happen, however, that a theologian may, according to the case,

raise questions regarding the timeliness, the form or even the contents of magisterial interventions.[6]

The CDF seems to equate *obsequium* with "the willingness to submit loyally," which can be present even when questions are being raised about the content of a magisterial statement. In later sections, the same document goes on to point out that the theologian may not consider himself exempt from adhering to any teaching that is not infallible (no. 33). "A theologian who is not disposed to think with the Church (*sentire cum Ecclesia*) contradicts the commitment he freely and knowingly made to teach in the name of the Church" (no. 37). In these passages, *obsequium* seems to be identified as a state of will or a habitual disposition rather than as actual assent in a particular case.

In spite of the great advances made by Vatican II, the Profession of Faith, *Ad Tuendam Fidem*, and the CDF "Commentary on the Profession of Faith," a number of problem areas remain. The following points may be mentioned as requiring further study on the part of theologians and further clarifications from the bishops and the Holy See.

The term "definitive," in its current theological usage, is relatively new. It was used in *Lumen Gentium* for the teaching of the ordinary and universal magisterium and for the response due to such teaching. It is now being used also for doctrines that are not proclaimed as revealed but are firmly taught by the supreme magisterium as intimately connected with revelation. The assent due to such teaching is likewise being described as "definitive." Some are asking whether the term "definitive," in these documents, is equivalent to "irreformable" and whether every definitive teaching is also infallible. It is also being asked whether the category of truths definitively taught (but not as matters of faith) corresponds to what was previously called the secondary object of infallibility.

Some have difficulty in seeing how the teaching on the ordination of women in *Ordinatio Sacerdotalis*—definitive though it be—could fit within the secondary object of infallibility. If the teaching is based simply on Scripture and Tradition, and not on naturally known premises, it would seem that it could not be certainly known except as a matter of faith. This would place the doctrine within the first category—that of revealed truth.[7]

Apart from a few very clear pronouncements from popes and councils, the decision about the theological note attaching to various doctrines has generally been left to approved Catholic authors. The consensus of theologians has been the principal method for identifying truths taught as revealed by the ordinary and universal magisterium. Theologians have been discussing for a century or more whether certain documents of the Holy See are infallible—for example, the Syllabus of Errors, the decision of Leo XIII on the invalidity of Anglican ordinations, the Oath against Modernism, and the solemn canonization of saints. New questions are raised about the infallible or *de fide* character of the Church's teaching on abortion, women's ordination, contraception, and euthanasia. While it may be urgent to settle the theological note of some of these doctrines, it may be legitimate and prudent to allow theological discussion to continue on others.

Further clarification about the Church's ability to teach matters of natural law infallibly would be desirable. According to one opinion, the capacity to teach the natural law with full authority falls within the Church's mission, since the observance of the natural law is required for salvation.[8] According to another opinion, the magisterium can speak with pastoral authority on all issues of the moral law. It can also speak infallibly on basic principles of the natural law that are also formally revealed; but the Church, it is said, has no power to speak infallibly about particular applications of the natural moral law unless these can be shown to be intimately or necessarily connected with revelation.[9]

It has traditionally been taught that anyone who deliberately doubts or denies a doctrine taught by the Church as contained in the deposit of faith is anathematized and incurs the canonical censure of heresy and is automatically excommunicated. Without rejecting this teaching, some are asking about the canonical status of Catholic Christians who in good faith question the revealed character of certain doctrines that seem to be rather remote from the central message of the Gospel. Under what conditions are such persons to be excluded from the sacramental life of the Church or deprived of office? This issue becomes quite practical when theology professors are required to make the current profession of faith.

It is asked, in addition, whether the communion of the Catholic with the Church is impaired by a failure to hold doctrines taught definitively but not taught as revealed. The commentary on the Profession of Faith seems to say that this is the case.[10] Does the commentary mean to imply that the canonical status of such persons is affected and that they are to be denied access to certain sacraments? Under what conditions is a Catholic "not in full communion with the Church"? Further study on the canonical and theological conceptions of communion might be able to shed light on these issues.

Questions such as those here mentioned have been present in the Church for a long time. Many of them do not urgently call for clear and immediate answers. But it might be well for organs such as the International Theological Commission to study some of them and to publish its findings in due course. The results of such studies could assist bishops in their dealings with theologians in Catholic universities in the United States and elsewhere.

# NOTES

1   Irenaeus, *Adv. Haer.* 4.26.2, speaks of those "who have received, together with their succession in the episcopate, the sure charism of truth, according to the good pleasure of the Father."

2   *Acta Synodalia Sacrosancti Concilii Oecumenici Vaticani II,* vol. III, no. I, 251; cf. Francis A. Sullivan, *Magisterium: Teaching Authority in the Catholic Church* (New York: Paulist Press, 1983), 132.

3   "Commentary on Profession of Faith's Concluding Paragraphs," no. 6, *Origins* 28 (July 16, 1998): 117.

4   John Paul II, apostolic letter *Ad Tuendam Fidem,* no. 3, *Origins* 28 (July 16, 1998): 115. I speak here of amendments to the Latin code. Corresponding emendations are made in *Ad Tuendam Fidem* to *Code of Canons of the Eastern Churches.*

5   Ibid.

6   CDF, "Instruction on the Ecclesial Vocation of the Theologian," *Origins* 20 (July 5, 1990): 122-23.

7   See the discussion of this point in the commentary on the Profession of Faith, no. 11, 118.

8   Umberto Betti, in his doctrinal commentary on the 1989 Profession of Faith, writes, "All that refers to the natural law, in that it is an expression of God's will, can also be included in the object of irreformable definitions, even though not of faith. For the same reason it also falls within the competence of the Church to interpret and to propose the natural law in virtue of her ministry of salvation," *L'Osservatore Romano* (English-language edition), no. 11 (March 13, 1989): 4.

9   This is the position of Francis A. Sullivan in "Some Observations on the New Formula for the Profession of Faith," *Gregorianum* 70 (1989): 552-54. See also his *Magisterium,* 136-52.

10  "Commentary on Profession of Faith's Concluding Paragraphs," no. 6, p. 117.

# Canadian Conference of Catholic Bishops

# IMPLICATIONS OF FEMINISM FOR CATHOLIC DOCTRINE

## HIS EMINENCE
## ALOYSIUS CARDINAL AMBROZIC

Feminism is one aspect of the far-reaching movement in our civilization which holds that many of the conditions and structures of individual and social life originate in culture rather than nature. The blossoming of science and technology, the reorganization of work and economic life, and the spread of new ideologies invite a revision of the relationship between men and women and of women's role in the family and in society.

Feminism wants to promote the dignity of women and advocate equality between men and women in various areas of everyday life and culture, particularly in the areas of family, work, and politics. Born in a world deeply marked, especially in the sphere of public life, by male hegemony and discrimination against women, feminism's stated aim is emancipation, struggle against the subjection of women and against the feeling of inferiority that centuries of male domination had inculcated in them.

In Christian circles, feminism has criticized severely a religious tradition whose ways of thinking and form of governance reproduced and consecrated the patriarchy and androcentrism of the surrounding cultures. Feminism rejects the image of woman who is at the service and disposition of the male, a permanent minor who could occasionally be dangerous, because of her charm and shrewdness. On a more positive note, feminism recalls the undertakings and intrepid action of many women in Israel and in the Church.

There are, indeed, many kinds of feminism in Christian circles. There is a reformist or moderate feminism allergic to the patriarchy of ecclesiastical structures but respectful of the Church hierarchy and the sacramental system. There is a revolutionary feminism which demands egalitarianism pure and simple in all spheres of the Church's life. For some groups within this trend, the Church is an incurably male structure from which women ought to depart. Yet another type of feminism engages in political action in favor of liberation and, at times, ecology.

What are the implications of feminism for Catholic thought? We will focus on doctrine, touching only indirectly on history or pastoral practice. Where can middle-of-the-road (moderate) feminism and Catholic teachings find agreement and mutual support? On the other hand, what is there in feminism which opposes, compromises, or contradicts the Church's doctrine?

## I. AGREEMENT AND MUTUAL SUPPORT

Women could not find an ally more clearly determined than the Church to recognize and defend their dignity. For the Church, a woman is, like man, a human person, consciousness and conscience, seat of perception and free will, open to the totality of being and goodness, an end not a means. Woman, like man, is a creature of God, made in his image and likeness, redeemed by the blood of Jesus Christ, the Son of God, inhabited by the Holy Spirit, called to eternal life in the embrace of the Trinity. It is through a woman and because of her femininity that the Son of God, consubstantial with the Father, is also consubstantial with us.

For Christian thought, woman is created equal to man, distinct and united in the image of God so that Genesis presents man and woman in the singular: "So God created man (*Adam*) in his own image, in the image of God he created him; male (*zakhar*) and female (*n'qebah*) he created them" (Gn 1:27). Man and woman are called upon jointly and equally to be fruitful and multiply, to fill the earth and subdue it (Gn 1:28). Equality, mutuality, interdependence, and common responsibility in facing the future and the world: these are the characteristics of the human couple in divine thought.

The domination of woman by man is not part of the Creator's design but rather an expression and consequence of sin. Indeed, for Christian doctrine as for feminism, domination by one sex over the other is not part of nature or any kind of destiny; it is the result and an aspect of the disorder introduced into the world by human will. "Every man experiences evil around him and within himself," says the *Catechism of the Catholic Church*. "This experience makes itself felt in the relationships between man and woman. Their union has always been threatened by discord, a spirit of domination, infidelity, jealousy, and conflicts that can escalate into hatred and separation" (no. 1606).

"According to faith the disorder we notice so painfully does not stem from the *nature* of man and woman, nor from the nature of their relations, but from *sin*. As a break with God, the first sin had for its first consequence the rupture of the original communion between man and woman. Their relations were distorted by mutual recriminations; their mutual attraction, the Creator's own gift, changed into a relationship of domination and lust. . ." (no. 1607).

In our time, the Church formulates the time-honored proclamation of the dignity and equality of woman, wounded by sin, in the language of protest and demand for action. Making reference to Pope John XXIII, who saw women's greater awareness of their proper dignity and their entry into public life as a sign of time, "the [1988] Synod

Fathers, when confronted with the various forms of discrimination and marginalization to which women are subjected simply because they are women, time and time again strongly affirmed the urgency to defend and to promote the *personal dignity of woman*, and consequently, her equality with man" (*Christifideles Laici* [CL], no. 49).

"If anyone has this task of advancing the dignity of women in the Church and society," the exhortation continues, "it is women themselves, who must recognize their responsibility as leading characters. There is still much effort to be done . . . to destroy that unjust and deleterious mentality which considers the human being as a thing, as an object to buy and sell, as an instrument for selfish interests or for pleasure only. Women themselves, for the most part, are the prime victims of such a mentality" (CL, no. 49).

In this respect, historians and sociologists are aware of how much the elevation of marriage to the rank of a sacrament, a special sign of the union of Christ and the Church, has contributed to the raising of the status of woman. They know how much the doctrine of the unity and indissolubility of marriage has done to free women from the condition of slave or instrument. No, a woman is not an element in a series or an interchangeable part!

If the cause of women has found support in the Church's doctrine and practice, it must be noted too that this new attention to women's qualities and talents enabled the Church to explore and deepen her own resources. Feminism has led to a new reading of the Bible and of Judeo-Christian history, in which women and women's values receive new emphasis. In particular, we have learned to appreciate how unusual Jesus was for his time and environment, with his freedom and independence and attitude of esteem and respect for women. The first Christian communities included prophetesses and deaconesses; there were women scholars and foundresses in the Patristic period and the Middle Ages; in modern times there has been no shortage of women who are religious and social activists and reformers. Today, women are deans of faculties of theology; they head delegations at international meetings and hold offices in diocesan chanceries.

It has been pointed out that besides the parent-child images serving to express the relationship between God and human beings as mainly one of submission and docility, the language of friendship, which comes so naturally to women, could give new life to many a biblical theme. "The metaphor of God as friend corresponds to the feminine ideal of 'communal personhood,' of mutual relations free of rivalry, where the self is realized through community."[1]

## II. Conflict and Divergence

Aside from areas of mutual support, feminism and Christian doctrine are in disagreement on some fundamental points. There is dispute, as we see it, on three major issues: the ontological significance of the difference between the sexes, the originality and historicity of Christianity, and the value of the symbolic or sacramental dimension of the body and sexuality.

An opening remark of an epistemological nature seems relevant. Modern feminism claims to be based above all on women's *experience*, that is, an experience of centuries of subjection, discrimination, and second-rate status inflicted on them by men. This experience is said to be so universal and profound that it seems inextricably tied to the one obvious reality that distinguishes women from men, namely, their gender. In an era when so many political, economic, and social realities, which hitherto seemed natural and unalterable, have been revealed as contingent, why not relativize the difference between the sexes as well, relegating it to the class of structures over which we have control and which we can therefore transform?

"The idea of a difference between the sexes that goes together with the equality of man and woman, has largely disappeared in our modern Western civilization," the German Episcopal Conference wrote recently (DC 91, 1994, p. 999). We are thus faced with the paradox of a feminist movement that has reduced the importance of femininity as such and puts forward a vision of the human being as uniform, abstract, and individualist.

It is no less paradoxical that it is the Church which must defend the ontological character of the difference between the sexes. The Church seeks to examine "the *anthropological foundation for masculinity and femininity* with the intent of clarifying woman's personal identity in relation to man, that is, a diversity yet mutual complementarity, not only as it concerns roles to be held and functions to be performed, but also, and more deeply, as it concerns her make-up and meaning as a person" (CL, no. 50).

The divine plan, as witnessed in the stories of creation, bodiliness, and specifically sexuality, expresses the relational character of persons; human reality is a *unity of two*. Physical relations and the transcendence of the subject are not foreign to one another, but indissolubly united. What the Second Vatican Council said about the human person as such is valid above all for the partners within the human couple: "Man is the only creature on earth that God has wanted for its own sake . . . he can fully discover his true self only in a sincere giving of himself" (*Gaudium et Spes*, no. 24). Openness to the other, and interdependence, are engraved in the very nature of human beings, both men and women.

The relationship between man and woman predates and is superior to any other association of persons, racial and ethnic groups included. This original mutuality is still the source of the continuance and progress of humanity. It should be no surprise that this first covenant of self-gift is the one that speaks to us most deeply about personal relationships in God himself and the relationships that God has created with humanity in Jesus Christ.

A second kind of difficulty for feminism in relation to Catholic doctrine arises from the nature of the Church, an institution completely dependent on the sovereign will of Christ, and not a natural society governed by our current systems of rights and laws. It is an institution which, moreover, takes its place in a gratuitous plan of salvation and in the specific history of a people chosen by God.

As was made clear by the debate on the exclusion of women from ordained ministry, feminism wishes to abolish the difference between the structures of civil life and those of the Christian Church: there is no room in the thought and life of the Church for the difference between the sexes. The very existence of a hierarchy manifests a system of male domination. Relationships between persons are to obey solely the criteria of efficiency.

It ought to be said, on the contrary, that the Church is part of a new, original, grace-given order called election, covenant, revelation, incarnation, redemption, the kingdom of God, new humanity built on the new Adam. Christ plays a unique and sovereign role in the new humanity. He has united humanity with God in the unity of one person; by means of his manner of acting and teaching, he shows God the Father to us; he has sacrificed himself for us and gave us rebirth in his death and resurrection. The Church thus owes him obedience and fidelity.

The entire Church thus rests completely in the *once and for all* (*ephaphax*) of the life of Christ and the community of the apostles. Though the Church is contemporary with every era and longs for its completion of the second coming, she remains forever linked to the earthly ministry of the Incarnate Word. It is essential that this *once and for all* be proclaimed not only in teaching but in the rites and structures. To this unique and *once for all* event the institution of the twelve is linked; the twelve are Jesus' representatives for all time. Through this group, Jesus continues his saving action in the entire history of the people of which the twelve are the leaders.

A third area of unease or conflict for feminism within the Christian community resides in the symbolic use of the language of the body, and in particular the difference of the sexes, in speaking of the Christian mystery. In a vision of the world which sees bodiliness and sexuality as secondary or external and merely functional, the analogy of the bridegroom and the bride can scarcely be seen as the primary expression of the relationship between Christ and the Church. A bodily coming of the Son of God into the world does not correspond to the vision according to which the human person is hardly more than consciousness and free will.

In Christian thought, as we have seen, bodiliness is symbolically transparent: marriage becomes the privileged expression of the mystery of God's gift of himself to humanity in the person of Jesus Christ. "A man leaves his father and mother and cleaves to his wife, and they become one flesh" (Gn 2:24). *This is a great mystery, and I mean in reference to Christ and the Church* (cf. Eph 5:32). What is new in the Gospel is that it is not only the wife who submits to the husband, but there is *"mutual subjection out of reverence for Christ"* (*Mulieris Dignitatem* [MD], no. 24; cf. Eph 5:21 ff.).

"In the Church, every human being—male and female—is the 'Bride,' in that he or she accepts the gift of the love of Christ the Redeemer, and seeks to respond to it with the gift of his or her own person. . . . The Bridegroom—the Son consubstantial with the Father as God— became the son of Mary; he became the 'son of man,' true man, a male. *The symbol of the Bridegroom is masculine.* This masculine symbol represents the human aspect of the divine love which God has for Israel, for the Church, and for all people" (MD, no. 25).

"The analogy of the Bridegroom and the Bride speaks of the love with which every human being—man and woman—is loved by God in Christ. But in the context of the biblical analogy and the text's interior logic, it is precisely the woman—the bride—who manifests this truth to everyone" (MD, no. 29). It is *the true order of love which constitutes woman's own vocation*" (MD, no. 30).

I conclude this paper with a set of wishes that the women's movement and the Catholic Church might express to one another.

To the women's movement, the Church might express the following desires:

- That women not allow the injustices they have suffered to blind them to the uniqueness and richness of their own condition as persons, engaged with men and equal with them in the progress of humanity.

- That women recognize with gratitude that their call is to be at the heart of every task and every function, in promoting and protecting human life, a fully human life.

- That as the symbol of the loving response to the love of God, women remind everyone of the primacy of sanctity over every structure and every distinction in the Church of Christ.

The movements for the defence and promotion of women might ask the Church the following:

- That the Church steadfastly take up the cause of women in the struggle against discrimination and abuse.

- That the Church read the Scriptures and Christian history in the light of the respect and consideration for women which Christ demonstrated in his teaching and actions.

- That the Church put forward images of man and woman with no trace of domination, where complementarity prevails and where the covenant between sexes is lived in esteem and respect.

## NOTE

1   Anne E. Carr, *Transforming Grace: Christian Tradition and Women's Experience* (New York: Continuum Pub Group, 1996).

# Australian Catholic Bishops' Conference

# THE PROBLEM OF
# HOMOSEXUALITY: DOCTRINAL
# ISSUES AND PASTORAL
# IMPLICATIONS

⸎

## MOST REVEREND ERIC D'ARCY

This is a large subject, ramifying into several interrelated disciplines. Rather than attempting to overview it discursively, I shall single out several elements crucial to the Church's doctrine on the matter, proceeding by way of example or quotation and reflection.

## I. DOCTRINES AND CONTEXT

Love the sinner, hate the sin![1] Some gay activists protest that it is "appallingly patronizing" to apply St. Augustine's aphorism to the matter of homosexuality. Yet it accurately headlines two of the prime essentials in the Church's doctrine about it.

On the one hand, the *Catechism of the Catholic Church* says,

> Basing itself on Sacred Scripture, which presents homo-
> sexual acts as acts of grave depravity, tradition has always
> declared that "homosexual acts are intrinsically disor-

dered."[2] They are contrary to the natural law. They close the sexual act to the gift of life. They do not proceed from a genuine affective and sexual complementarity. Under no circumstances can they be approved. (no. 2357)

On the other hand, the Congregation for the Doctrine of the Faith (CDF), while reiterating that doctrine, also insists,

It is deplorable that homosexual persons have been and are the object of violent malice in speech and in action. Such treatment deserves condemnation from the Church's pastor wherever it occurs. It reveals a kind of disregard for others which endangers the fundamental principles of a healthy society. The intrinsic dignity of every person must always be respected in word, in action and in law.[3]

One cannot discuss the Church's doctrines in a cultural vacuum. We must not discuss her doctrines about homosexuality in isolation from today's First-World cultural mores. Let me point to three elements in those mores.

1.  Our people are children and grandchildren of the modern Sexual Revolution. Its slogans are potent in every peer group, from the demotic "whatever turns you on," to the more staid, "The rightful autonomy of the human individual entitles each person to seek sexual gratification in whatever mode is found to be rewarding."

Most deflating of all, in many a younger group hearing the Church's doctrine on chastity expounded, is the cheerful insistence that *sex is just good fun.* "Why so heavy about all this? Why make such a big deal of it? It's just good fun."

And yet, in many groups, one or two members reveal a deep-seated conviction that there is more to sex than physical pleasure: that truly human sexuality is meant to involve an element of affectionate mutual self-giving. And how often does a pastor hear, from a depth of misery, the age-old cry, "I thought he loved me."

2.   There is throughout the West a ubiquitous Subjectivism and Relativism, especially with regard to religion and morals. In *Veritatis Splendor* (VS), Pope John Paul II remarked on the tendency, constantly taking deeper root over the last two hundred years, to exalt freedom to such an extent that it becomes the absolute source of values. He argues, "At this rate the inescapable claims of *truth* would disappear, giving way to a criterion of sincerity, authenticity and 'being at peace' with oneself," so much so that some have come to adopt a radically subjectivistic conception of moral judgement" (VS, nos. 32, 1).

All too commonly a firm judgment of "true" or "false" is evaded and replaced with such questions as, "Do you feel comfortable with this?"

Two things played some part in preventing such relativism from becoming all-conquering in our culture. First, in 1946, the war crime trials rejected the claim of some perpetrators "never to have acted against conscience or the law of their own land." Second, in 1948, was the United Nations Universal Declaration of Human Rights. Fifty years later it remains astonishing that such a list of specific rights was unanimously recognized and endorsed. They were conferred by no parliament or congress, but arise from human nature itself. As Clifford Longley recently wrote, "Human rights are moral concepts before they are legal ones."[4]

More recently, we can welcome growing elements of Moral Objectivism among serious social and political commentators. Melanie Phillips is a case in point. Writing in the leftish secular weekly *The Observer*, she warmly welcomed "the new encyclical, magnificently named *Veritatis Splendor*." She spoke sardonically of those nervous Catholics for whom "the Pope is of course the supreme pontiff of political incorrectness." Firmly she declared that "the encyclical's broader and deeper argument goes to the heart of the modern dilemma that affects us all. Duty and responsibility have been thrown out of the window because one person's truth is as valid as anyone else's."

This ethical relativism has subverted political culture as well. Contrary to the bad press they get, only absolute moral values can truly protect individual freedom from being trampled underfoot and produce a society based on principles of justice, solidarity, honesty, and openness.[5]

Finally, and even more significant for the long run, is the rise of a strong new movement within professional Anglo-American philosophy called "Moral Realism." We must look at it later.

3. Items in a modern society's mores can be quite ephemeral. The novelist Francis King was recently reviewing a new biography of the winner of the 1948 Nobel Prize for Literature, André Gide, whose history King contrasted with that of Oscar Wilde who was jailed for sodomy.

Gide's close heterosexual friends looked on his pederasty as nothing more than an unfortunate foible, more reprehensible than taking to the bottle, less reprehensible than shoplifting. In the last ten years or so, the Western world's whole attitude to pederasty has become infinitely tougher, so that if Gide and Oscar Wilde were living today it would be Gide who would go to prison and be ostracized, and Wilde who would eventually be awarded a Nobel Prize.[6]

This is quite a volte-face—or rather, double volte-face—in our mores. Can you imagine the Church following suit—anxiously, eagerly, re-writing this, that, and the other doctrine so as to keep in tune with the latest aria of the zeitgeist?

# II. Scripture and Tradition, Conscience and Moral Truth

"*Traditio, sacra nitens Scriptura*: Tradition, basing itself on sacred Scripture, has always taught. . . ." Both the *Catechism* and *On the Pastoral Care of Homosexual Persons* (CDF 1986), in addressing the question of homosexuality, refer to the usual five or six passages in Scripture; but they are not quarrying the Bible in pursuit of knock-down arguments from proof-texts. Some Bible Christians may proceed like that, but it is not the Church's way.

For one thing, she would not be satisfied simply to consider those texts one by one in mutual isolation. Despite the great diversity of social, cultural, and religious context in which they were written, she recognizes across them all a constant moral condemnation—not a mere taboo—of what today are called homosexual acts; but there is much more to it than that. The Church always reflects upon the whole Scriptural canon. In this matter she starts from the Genesis account of the creation, which culminates in its two accounts of the creation of man and woman and the inaugural complementarity of the two sexes.

But of course the actual process is much richer than any *sola Scriptura* approach, however sophisticated. The Church proceeds along lines memorably set out by Vatican II:

> It is not from Sacred Scripture alone that the Church draws her certainty about all that has been revealed. Sacred Tradition and Sacred Scripture are both to be accepted and both to be venerated with equal loyalty and reverence. Sacred Tradition and Sacred Scripture form one sacred deposit of the Word of God committed to the Church. (*Dei Verbum* [DV], nos. 9-10)

Being traditional does not mean confining oneself to repeating past formulae; it means being recognizably in organic continuity with the forms of understanding which the Church, under the guidance of the Holy Spirit, has been developing over the two thousand years of Catholic life. She sees her teaching on homosexuality in a rich doctrinal context involving the nuptial significance of the human body, the nature of relationships, especially friendship, the covenantal and sacramental character of marriage, the symbolism and meaning of sexuality, the place of self-giving in a life of chastity, whether married or single.

Data given by that long Spirit-guided process—they are not merely logical conclusions entailed by premises arrived at earlier—are articulated as follows by CDF 1986:

> It is only in the marital relationship that the use of the sexual faculty can be morally good. This of course applies to any sexual genital activity between persons not married to each other. CDF 1986 spells it out with regard to such activity between persons of the same sex: To choose someone of the same sex for one's sexual activity is to annul the rich symbolism and meaning, not to mention the goals, of the Creator's sexual design. Homosexual activity expresses no such complementary union, capable of transmitting life; and so it thwarts the call to a life of that form of self-giving which, the Gospel says, is the essence of Christian living. (no. 7)

The demands of chastity are difficult enough for many a Christian, heterosexual or homosexual, even one who has grown up well educated and formed in the twin life and teaching of Scripture and Tradition. What of the person of good will who has been blessed with no such formation? To respond to this question it is natural to think of a remarkable teaching of Vatican II.

*Gaudium et Spes* (GS) was written twenty years after World War II ended, yet the Council Fathers had to grieve over new and terrible weapons, internecine killing, guerilla warfare, new methods of deceit and terrorism: all afflicting so much of the human race. For all the celebratory optimism running through that final Council document, the Fathers declared:

> Contemplating this sorry state of humanity, the Council wishes above all things else to recall the permanent binding force of universal natural law and its all-embracing principles. Conscience itself gives ever more emphatic voice to these principles. Therefore actions which deliberately conflict with those principles, as well as orders commanding such actions, are criminal, and blind obedience cannot excuse those who obey them. (no. 79)

Such robust Moral Objectivism, and the refusal to concede untrammelled rights to conscience, will delight many people in the case of those particular activities. But not all of those same people will be equally enthusiastic when that objectivism is applied to sexual activity.

Natural Law reflection upon the nature of the human person, and of human choice, has always led the Church to declare that homosexual genital activity is objectively contrary to Natural Law. This has been reiterated recently by the declaration *On Certain Questions Concerning Sexual Ethics* (CDF 1975) (nos. III.3, IV), CDF 1986, the *Catechism of the Catholic Church* (no. 2357), and the 1995 re-issue of CDF 1986 with a new preface by the Archbishop-Secretary of the Congregation and a new introduction by the Cardinal-Prefect.

*There are knowable moral truths*: this assumption has always been basic in the Magisterium's metaethic. Providentially, interest in that same assumption has led to the rise of Moral Realism:[7] a cluster of moral theories which constitute an important recent development in

Anglo-American moral *philosophy*. A vein of cognitivism/objectivism runs through them. In moral *theology*, however, there is a trend which would take us back to the days when mainstream English-speaking moral philosophy was subjectivist or "non-cognitivist."

We have already seen how Pope John Paul II noted that a two-hundred-years-old tendency in our culture could displace considerations of *truth* from moral thought and discourse. Recently Joseph Cardinal Ratzinger took this line of thought a little further:

> In today's cultural environment, and especially in connexion with questions of Catholic morality, the Church has need to challenge the viewpoint which asserts that a moral judgement is true, or "valid," simply by virtue of the fact that it is in accord with one's personal conscience.[8]

The tendency thus identified by the Holy Father and the Cardinal may be seen at work all too widely in the general scene of our cultural mores, in the social sciences, and indeed in a major stream of Catholic religious educationism. It is therefore providential that such a movement as Moral Realism has risen so strongly in anglophone philosophy.

"You cannot infer values from facts" was a dogma inherited by our culture from the secular enlightenment. Philosophers trace its first draft to the young David Hume's famous "No Ought from Is" paragraph of 1739. From 1903, any claim to infer values from facts was condemned as committing "the Naturalistic Fallacy." Freshers came up to university from government schools saying, "Of course facts are objective; values are only subjective, aren't they?"—almost apologetic for stating so trite an axiom. With the coming of Experientialist Model catechetics, Catholic high school graduates were soon saying similar things.

In academic philosophy the first really damaging attack on the claim that there is an unbridgeable logical gap between fact and value, and on the subjectivism ("non-cognitivism") that it fed, was made by Philippa Foot,[9] an Oxford don who became professor of philosophy at UCLA. So convincing were her arguments, and those of many other philosophers subsequently, that forty years later it was enough for Hilary Putnam of Harvard, delivering the prestigious Gifford lectures, simply to remark that "the idea of a sharp cut between facts' and values' is deeply wrong."[10]

Throughout the rest of our culture, however, great numbers of people are heavily, though often unwittingly, possessed by the conviction that in religion and morality there can be no truth, but only "values"—perhaps personal ones, perhaps social, but at any rate not objectively true. Hence it has become commonplace to hear people avoiding the words *good* or *bad*; instead, they say *positive* or *negative*. They shrink from saying *right* or *wrong*; instead, they say *appropriate* or *inappropriate* (often, in a tone of indignation, "totally inappropriate"). Worst of all, many quite flinch away from saying *true* or *false*; they take refuge in evasion words, especially *valid* or *invalid*.

It is startling to see non-cognitivist assumptions at work here and there in Catholic Moral Theology. A case in point is the recent book of the English theologian Rev. Kevin Kelly, *New Directions in Sexual Ethics*. He visited CAFOD's (Catholic Fund for Overseas Development) AIDS projects in Uganda, Thailand, and the Philippines. He was almost overwhelmed, seeing for himself the "enormous horror of the pandemic," and was generously moved to make some priestly contribution towards alleviating it with what he knows and does best—Moral Theology. Unfortunately, in a book full of quite beautiful pastoral insight and intent, one of the major positions Rev. Kelly reaches is the following inference from his own account of Conscience:

Within the Roman Catholic Church, for instance, this means that no official teaching on sexual ethics can oblige a Catholic to act against their conscience or to accept as true any ethical ruling of the Church which they conscientiously believe not to be true. It also means that a person is abdicating their moral responsibility as a human person if they decline to follow their own convinced conscience purely because a Church directive on sexual ethics forbids them to do what they know they really should do.[11]

This of course is quite at odds with Vatican II. *Gaudium et Spes* declares that Conscience is one's most secret core, one's sanctuary, where one is alone with God whose voice echoes in its depths. Some people have taken this as approval of subjectivism; but the very same paragraph goes on to say, "the more that right conscience holds sway, the more do persons and groups turn aside from blind choice and strive to be guided by the objective standards of moral conduct" (GS, no. 16). And elsewhere Vatican II—in *Dignitatis Humanae*, the very declaration which so famously upheld the right to religious freedom—insisted on the constant duty of a Catholic conscience vis-à-vis the teaching authority of the Church:

In forming conscience Christ's faithful must carefully attend to the sacred and certain doctrine of the Church. For the Catholic Church is, by the will of Christ, the teacher of truth. It is her duty to proclaim and teach with authority that truth which is Christ Himself, and at the same time to declare and confirm by her authority those principles of the moral order which spring from human nature itself. (no. 14)

Rev. Kelly's book was warmly welcomed by Rev. James F. Keenan, SJ. He found that "the real genius of Kelly's work is the very positive reading that he gives to the tradition." He summarized one argument in particular:

[Rev. Kelly] argues that before we examine whether another person's particular sexual activity is right, we as members of the Church must ask ourselves two prior questions. First, have we adequately entertained the Church's principle of justice so as to apply it universally? Do we treat women as equal to men? Do we accept homosexuals as equal to heterosexuals?

Secondly, if we do, then do we consider the testimony of their experiences to be as valid as the experience of the celibate males who have formulated present teachings?[12]

But surely this is something of an *ignoratio elenchi*. A Pope does not derive his authority for teaching Church doctrine from an alleged superior "validity" of his personal "experiences."

Just as a Pope does not *experience* the neuronal changes constantly occurring in his brain, he does not *experience* the bread's changing into the body of Our Lord at Mass. He knows the fact of the neuronal changes, not from personal experience of them, but from reports of neuroscientific research familiar enough to any educated person. He teaches the truth of transubstantiation, not from some personal experience, but from all that the Holy Spirit has done in the course of fulfilling the promise, *"when the Spirit of truth comes, he will guide you into all the truth"* (Jn 16:13) [italics added].

As for the challenge, "Do we consider the testimony of [women's and homosexuals'] experiences to be as valid [*sic*] as the experiences of the celibate males who have formulated present teachings?": this must be met head-on. Vatican II made no bones about it:

In maintaining, practicing and professing the faith that has been handed on there should be a special harmony between the bishops and the faithful. But the task of authoritatively interpreting the Word of God, whether in its written form or in the form of tradition, has been entrusted solely to the living Magisterium of the Church, whose authority is exercised in the name of Jesus Christ." (DV, no. 10)

Of course if one has, supervening upon a difficult decision to follow Catholic moral doctrine against the prevailing social mores or the "inclinations of the flesh," a supportive religious or moral experience that is a welcome and most helpful bonus. But it is an uncovenanted mercy; one cannot count on it, nor be surprised at its absence. It is not the stuff of moral decision-making.

There are knowable moral truths: interest in this was one source of the rise of the movement called Moral Realism in English-speaking professional philosophy. On the other hand, Sabina Lovibond came to it through the refutation of the old slogan, "Facts are objective, values only subjective," by way of the later Wittgenstein's account of language as metaphysically homogeneous.[13] By 1994 it took Margaret Little of Bryn Mawr seventeen closely printed pages simply to set out the main proponents and the main propositions of the main versions of Moral Realism.[14] She too recognizes "fertile recent developments in theories of Truth, Semantics and Justification" as another spur to the rise of Moral Realism.

Marc Platts's is a classic statement of the Moral Realism thesis:

> [Moral judgments are] factually cognitive, presenting claims about the world which can be assessed (like any other factual belief) as true or false; their truth or falsity are as much possible objects of human knowledge as are any other factual claims about the world.[15]

Platts goes on to deal with the relationship between moral and non-moral facts, driving home the point that both kinds are *facts*, factual truths about the real world. Significantly he calls the chapter on morality, not "Moral Realism," but "Moral *Reality*."

It will be a sad failure to read the signs of the times if we—at least we Anglophones—fail to see any potential connection between the insistent objectivism in the teaching of the Magisterium, and the rise of Moral Realism in professional English-speaking philosophy. It is surely providential that such a strain of moral Cognitivism should be developing among us at the very moment when relativist and subjectivist theories are being invoked against a great deal of the Church's counter-cultural moral doctrine.

## III. *"Haec Propensio, Obiective Inordinata"*

How does one convey in English the full and exact connotation of this expression in no. 2358 of the *editio typica* of the *Catechism of the Catholic Church*?

Homosexual acts are gravely immoral, indeed "depraved." A homosexual orientation is not; nevertheless it is not morally irrelevant.

*On the Pastoral Care of Homosexual Persons* (1986) recalls that, in the discussion which followed the publication of *On Certain Questions Concerning Sexual Ethics (Persona Humanæ)*, "An overly benign interpretation was given to the homosexual condition itself. Some went so far as to call it neutral, or even good" (no. 3). Later it states that "increasing numbers of ·people today, even within the Church, are bringing enormous pressure to bear on the Church to accept the homosexual condition as though it were not disordered, and to condone homosexual activity" (no. 8).

The most sustained and articulate case of this in Australia is made by Rev. Maurice Shinnick's book, *This Remarkable Gift*. The title accurately indicates a recurring theme throughout its pages: homosexuality is claimed to be a gift, a grace, a blessing, a calling, from God— for this is how it is experienced by some homosexuals, and that is how it is regarded by some theologians.

But of course the fact that something is experienced by some people as a gift cannot make it so if, objectively, it is disabling or disorienting; for instance, many a young German was given an *experience* of meaning in life, and of call to selfless duty, by the Hitler youth movement. To say that homosexuality is good because some people "experience" it as such is to beg the question.

The claim is vulnerable also to the counterclaim that there are people who "experience" homosexuality as a curse rather than a blessing, a debt rather than a gift.

A central thesis of Rev. Shinnick's book is that homosexuality is "integral to the nature and personhood of gay men and lesbian women" and therefore good, not a disorder. Rev. Shinnick claims that today, increasingly, Christian and spiritual gay people "value their sexuality as a gift. In this gift they are discovering a new dimension of spirituality because their sexuality is fundamental to their ability to relate to others in love" (p. 126).

Against this is the fact that, as an Iris Murdoch character says, "being homosexual doesn't determine a man's whole character any more than being heterosexual does."[16] All sorts of things may appear "integral to one's nature and personhood" without being directly willed by God, even permissively, or being the result of grace; they may be the result of original sin, of biology, of upbringing, or of personal choice, rather than of divine conferring.

Furthermore, if homosexuality were good in itself, a gift from God, the Scriptural and Traditional prohibitions of its expression in homosexual *acts* would be incoherent. One would expect, instead, "foundation myths" for homosexual activity, such as the Genesis account provides for the origins of heterosexual marriage and the family. One would expect vocational commands to homosexual couples, parallel to those given to heterosexual men and women, to cleave and become one flesh. One would expect the sacramentalizing of homosexual acts in some way parallel to the marital ceremony; and so on. As a matter of fact, some of these things are in fact being promised or sought by contemporary homosexual lobbyists—for example, same-sex marriage, the creation of corresponding myths. But these would be recognized at once for what they were: modern inventions, without support from the Judaeo-Christian tradition.

Does the English word "disorder" faithfully, successfully, convey the meaning of what the Magisterium teaches?

It is true that the English *Catechism* (1994) at no. 2537 has "disordered" for the French *Catéchisme*'s (1992) "*désordonnés*." But it is a familiar fact that to transliterate is often to translate erroneously: to render the French "*actuel*" as "actual," for instance, or the Italian "*editore*" routinely as "editor"—worse still, "*convitti*" as "convicts." The Latin in the *editio typica* (1997) has "*inordinatos*": to translate this as "inordinate" would be a straightforward error. And after all, in modern English, does "disorder" have the same intention and extension as "disordered"?

"Language is Power": these questions cannot be brushed aside as *lis de verbis potiusquam de re*. Rev. Shinnick no doubt chose the title *This Remarkable Gift* in order to encourage homosexual persons not to be ashamed of their sexual orientation and to celebrate and glory in it as, he seeks to argue, a remarkable gift from God.

We need therefore to compare the *editio typica* Latin of no. 2358 with three earlier vernacular versions.

The French (1992) reads, "*Ils ne choisissent pas leur condition homosexuelle. . . .*" The Italian (1992) has "*Costoro non scelgono la loro condizione omosessuale. . . .*" The English (1994) is "They do not choose their homosexual condition. . . ." Each of the three could be taken as a literal translation of the other two. But the Latin (1997) at the same place reads, "*Haec propensio, obiective inordinata. . . .*"

This is revealing. Four points deserve to be noted.

First, the term "*obiective*" is not only making a philosophical and theological point. At all times the Congregation and the *Catechism* scrupulously refrain from passing judgment on a person's "subjective" state of heart or soul.

Second, the word which in the previous sentence was "*tendances*," "*tendenze*," "tendencies," "*tendentiae*," is in the next sentence referred to as a "*condition*," "*condizione*," "condition" in the three vernacular versions: but in the Latin it is called a "*propensio*." Perhaps this change in the Latin was made out of sensitivity to some objections that the phrase "the homosexual condition" refers to much more than an individual's sexual orientation; rather, some argued, it embraces the whole homosexual "scene" in all its manifestations, initiatives, and self-inquiries, both individual and communal. A different line of this objection comes from those who object to any suggestion that homosexuality is not perfectly normal.

Third, the Latin simply omits the statement, common to the other three, that most homosexual persons "do not choose their homosexual condition. . . ."

Fourth, there is a phrase in the Latin of which there is no trace in the other three: "*obiective inordinata: Haec propensio, obiective inordinata.*"

This is significant. The "*inordinatos*" in no. 2357 is not synonymous with the "*inordinata*" in no. 2358. In no. 2357 it has a meaning on a par with "depraved," objectively immoral. In no. 2358 it carries no such suggestion; yet it is certainly not morally irrelevant.

Hence the parallel with the Council of Trent's teaching which has often been noted. The *concupiscentia vel fomes* which remains after baptism is referred to by St. Paul as "sin" (Rom 6:12ff, 7:7, 20)—not that it is, in those re-born, "sin" in the true and strict *sense—vere et proprie*—but because *"ex peccato est ad peccatum inclinat"* (Denziger-Schönmetzer, 1973, no. 1515). It was bold of an ecumenical council to declare roundly that St. Paul was not using "sin" in the true and strict sense. Equally, the *Catechism* in no. 2358 is using the term "disordered" analogically.

All the same, *omnis comparatio claudicat*: there are indeed rewarding points of similarity between the two analogies; but there is an essential difference. Every human person—with one glorious exception—is conceived in original sin and, having attained the age of rational responsibility, succumbs to personal sin. But it is not the case that every human person of homosexual propensity indulges in homosexual genital activity. Powerful, endlessly repeated, messages in the media would have us accept *as a truth universally acknowledged* that everyone actively follows their sexual inclinations. This is simply not true.

There is another semantic difficulty about translating *"inordinata"* as "disordered." In scholastic Latin *"ordinari," "ordinatus,"* and so on are systematically loaded with teleological implications: *telos* in the strict sense of the built-in end towards which an organ or an activity is internally oriented by its nature—*finis operis*, not just *finis operantis*. Unfortunately, the English "ordered" does not bear this semantic loading; "ordered towards" may be recognized as doing so—stipulatively, so to say—by those trained in scholastic thought, but not by the ordinary educated English-speaker. This is one of our difficulties when expounding Catholic teaching on sexuality and married chastity in terms of procreative and unitive "ends": "meaning" and better still "significance," may make a different point, but they do so more successfully.

Be all that as it may, I know of no English word that gets closer to the Latin than "disorder," though I shall be delighted to learn of one. Of course, it must not be a term devoid of moral reference.

# IV. PASTORAL IMPLICATIONS

This whole matter needs to be addressed with great seriousness. We have to deal with it as communities, as Church members, as families, as individual Christian persons. It is the subject of much misinformation, prejudice, rancour, even some violence; in the present climate people's lives are at risk, their freedom and security and reputations at stake. Homosexual persons are made in the image of God; their human dignity is recognized by the Christian faith; theology should enrich their lives; full communion with herself is the Church's desire for every one of them. There is a growing awareness of the diversity of homosexuality (or "homosexualities") and a need for greater study of its causes. There must be respectful and genuine dialogue with, and justice and inclusiveness towards, homosexual persons. As much as any other Catholics who take their faith-life seriously, they must be helped to develop and maintain virtuous characters and healthy friendships; the strengths in their characters and relationships must be appreciated and built upon. The contemporary AIDS crises must never be presented as a divine judgment; confessors must be aware of the reduced freedom, compulsions, and sensitivities of some homosexual penitents; preachers must be delicate with their congregations.

It is beyond the length allotted to this paper to address each of those issues. It is much further beyond my own personal limitations. I confine myself therefore to a word about each of four issues: the first two concern more directly Catholic homosexual persons, the other two concern more directly us Bishops as teachers and trustees of Catholic truth.

1. The whole world gasped when, on hundreds of millions of television sets, Pope John Paul II here in California was seen to lift a baby out of her little bed, and embrace her, and kiss her, and gently lay her down again with his blessing. She was stricken with AIDS. For huge numbers of people it was a defining action.

Entirely regardless of how the HIV virus has been contracted, any person afflicted with AIDS must have the best therapy and palliative care available: "Today the Church provides a badly needed context for the care of a human person when she refuses to consider that person as a 'heterosexual' or a 'homosexual' insisting rather that every human being has the same fundamental identity: creature of God and by grace his child and heir to eternal life" (*On the Pastoral Care of Homosexual Persons*, no. 16). As for the pastoral aspects, the Congregation also writes, "The remarkable concern and goodwill exhibited by many clergy and religious in their pastoral care of homosexual persons is truly admirable. These devoted ministers may be quite certain that they are faithfully following the will of the Lord by encouraging the homosexual person to lead a chaste life and by affirming that person's God-given dignity and worth" (no. 13).

2.  A pastorally prudential criterion implied by the doctrine is also stated very emphatically by the Congregation: while the provision of pastoral care for homosexual persons is warmly encouraged, no program will be authentic if it includes organizations in which homosexual persons associate with each other without clearly acknowledging the immorality of homosexual genital activity. In unusually strong words, the Congregation declares that "departure from the Church's teaching, or silence about it, in the effort to provide pastoral care, is neither caring nor pastoral"; this would be introducing such people into proximate occasions of sin (*On the Pastoral Care of Homosexual Persons*, no. 15).

That was in 1986. In 1999 Basil Cardinal Hume of Westminster applied it to a particular pastoral situation. A Catholic support group for homosexuals, Quest, was excluded from the English *Catholic Directory* for 1999. He explained his reasons in a letter to Quest's chairman. To be included, he wrote, "The assumption must be that [the organization] accepts the Church's teaching set out in a manner that is not ambiguous." In his quietly firm way, he gave his reasons for believing that this was no longer the case with Quest. For instance, in 1995 a substantial percentage of members passed a motion that "the full expression of same-sex love within a personal relationship is entirely compatible with Catholic Faith"; and the *Quest Chronicle* declared that "this amounts to a statement from Quest." Again in 1998, at a special general meeting of members, the national committee proposed a resolution to remove ambiguities in the Quest constitution "by making clear that one of the purposes of Quest was to encourage acceptance of the need to live chaste lives in accordance with the Church's teaching." But this was rejected, albeit by a small majority.

The Cardinal expressed the hope that Quest could soon be restored to the Catholic directory; but, he said, "this can be so only if you resolve the single point at issue by a suitable amendment to your constitution. It must make clear that part of the main purpose of Quest is to encourage its members to an acceptance of the need to live chaste lives in accordance with the Church's teaching. Furthermore it would also be necessary to revise that part of your press release concerning the encouragement and recognition of loving same-sex partnerships.'"

3.  Pope Paul VI said that the art of the apostle is a risky one. A few hours after Pope John Paul II had embraced the little Californian AIDS victim, shrill voices were condemning him for preaching in modern America a principle as old as the Gospel: vis-à-vis, sexual genital activity is morally lawful only between husband and wife; in other cases it is, objectively, gravely immoral. This applies to heterosexual persons and to homosexual persons. For great numbers, of whatever sexual orientation, the reaction was that of the crowd at Capernaum: "This is a hard saying. Who could accept it?" (Jn 6:60).

At the start of the century, that moral principle was widely accepted as self-evidently true throughout the Christian West. At the end of the century, it is widely rejected as self-evidently false throughout the post-Christian West. The magnitude of the challenge to preach it uncompromisingly in today's cultural climate will prompt many a bishop to think of St. Paul's charge to Timothy: "*I charge you: preach the word and, welcome or unwelcome, insist on it. Refute falsehood, correct error, call to obedience; be unfailing in patience and in teaching. The time is coming when people will not endure sound teaching. . .*" (2 Tm 4:2-3). Some of us certainly will recognize in ourselves more of Timothy than of Paul.

Today's Bishops from North America and Australasia can contrast the pastoral and cultural situation in which we have been entrusted with the mission of preaching and teaching Catholic moral doctrine, with the situation of our predecessors one hundred years ago. True, organizationally and economically we are far better placed for the mission than they were. But they did not have to preach a Gospel and teach a sexual morality so sharply unwelcome in the cultural mores of the time, as we must. And our predecessors did not have to teach a morality which was under attack from a significant minority of their own theologians. Let me conclude with one remark about this last situation.

4.   Evelyn Waugh once wrote that theology is "the mainspring and deep abiding channel of human thought: the branch of writing which . . . even today is second I believe for *quantity*, in all branches of publishing, and for *quality* commands the deepest intellects and the sharpest wits; the science which deals with the purpose and destination of the spirit of man."[17]

Of all the Catholic theologians whom I have known personally, there was never one who was a mere professional (as was Fanny Logan's professor-of-theology husband in Nancy Mitford's novels). They have all seen their life's work as a vocation within the Church's teaching mission and are proud to be numbered among "those who hold and teach the Catholic Faith that comes to us from the Apostles" (Roman Canon, Eucharistic Prayer I).

But there is a tension at the heart of the Catholic theologian's vocation. Both factors in this tension have been memorably remarked on by John Cardinal Newman.

On the one hand, theologians who are faithful Catholics are beholden to the authoritative teachings of the Church in a way that their colleagues are not. This is somewhat parallel to an artist's moral obligation as described by Benedetto Croce, perhaps the greatest philosopher of aesthetics in our century. He insisted that the artist, even at the height of artistic creativity, never ceases to be subject to the moral law because the artist never ceases to be a human being. The corresponding thing holds for the faithful Catholic theologian who, even when theologizing at full stretch, never ceases to be a faithful Catholic.

Newman states this uncompromisingly, in all its glory. He venerates the pursuit of truth by secular academics and scientists; but he firmly contrasts it with

> that true religious zeal which leads theologians to keep the Ark of the Covenant in every letter of its dogma as a tremendous deposit for which they are responsible. In this curious skeptical world, such sensitiveness is the only means by which the treasure of faith can be kept inviolate.[18]

On the other hand, the theologian is to be far more than a chronicler or a historian of doctrine, or a devotional commentator on it. Newman boldly says,

> There is no greater mistake, surely, than to suppose that a revealed truth precludes originality in the treatment of it . . . a re-assertion of what is old with a luminousness of explanation which is new, is a gift inferior only to that of Revelation itself.[19]

May we, Bishops and theologians, work confidently together for the resolving of this tension *sicut oportet*.

# NOTES

1   "*Cum dilectione hominum et odio vitiorum,*" St. Augustine, Letter 211, in Migne, P.L. (1845), vol. 33. The English translation/paraphrase as quoted, "Love the sinner, hate the sin," has established itself as an aphorism in its own right.

2   Congregation for the Doctrine of the Faith (CDF), declaration *On Certain Questions Concerning Sexual Ethics (Persona Humanæ),* 29.12.

3   CDF, letter to the bishops of the Catholic Church *On the Pastoral Care of Homosexual Persons,* re-issued with official introduction in 1995, no. 10.

4   Clifford Longley, *London Tablet* 27:3 (1999): 422.

5   Melanie Phillips, *London Observer* 10:x (1993).

6   Frances King, review of *André Gide,* by Alan Sheridan, *The Spectator* 10:24 (1998): 46.

7   Margaret Little, "Moral Realism I," *Philosophical Books* (July 1994): 145.

8   Address to Australian Bishops, 19:xi (1998).

9   Philippa Foot, "Moral Arguments," *Mind* (October 1958).

10  Hilary Putnam, *Renewing Philosophy* (Cambridge, Mass.: Harvard University Press, 1995), 135.

11  Kevin Kelly, *New Directions in Sexual Ethics* (London: Geoffrey Chapman, 1997), 170.

12  *London Tablet* 4:4 (1998).

13  Cf. Sabina Lovibond, *Realism and Imagination in Ethics* (Oxford: Blackwell, 1983), especially sections 1-19.

14  Margaret Little, "Moral Realism I & II," *Philosophical Books* (July and October 1994).

15  Mark Platts, *Ways of Meaning* (London: Henley; Boston: Routledge and Kegan Paul, 1979), 243.

16  Iris Murdoch, *A Fairly Honourable Defeat* (London: Penguin, 1972), 15-16.

17  Donat Gallagher, ed., *The Essays, Articles and Reviews of Evelyn Waugh* (London: Methuen, 1983), 402.

18  John Henry Newman, *On Consulting the Faithful,* ed. John Coulson (London: Geoffrey Chapman, 1961), 6.

19  John Henry Newman, "The Benedictine Schools," *Historical Sketches II* (London: Longmans Green, 1885), 475-6. For a consideration of the tension exemplified by these two quotations from Cardinal Newman, in another context, cf. Eric D'Arcy, "Towards the First Golden Age?" *The Australasian Catholic Record* (July 1997).